Dear Reader:

The book you are about to read is the latest bestseller from St. Martin's True Crime Library, the imprint *The New York Times* calls "the leader in true crime!" Each month, we offer you a fascinating account of the latest, most sensational crime that has captured the national attention. *The Milwaukee Murders* delves into the twisted world of Jeffrey Dahmer, one of the most savage serial killers of our time; *Death of a Little Princess* details the tragic story of little JonBenét Ramsey; *Lethal Lolita* gives you the *real* scoop on the deadly love affair between Amy Fisher and Joey Buttafuoco; *Whoever Fights Monsters* takes you inside the special FBI team that tracks serial killers; *Unanswered Cries* is the story of a detective who tracked a killer for a year, only to discover it was someone he knew and trusted; *Bad Blood* is the story of the notorious Menendez brothers and their sensational trials; *Sins of the Mother* details the sad account of Susan Smith and her two drowned children; *Fallen Hero* details the riveting tragedy of O. J. Simpson and the case that stunned a nation.

St. Martin's True Crime Library gives you the stories *behind* the headlines. Our authors take you right to the scene of the crime and into the minds of the most evil murderers to show you what really makes them tick. St. Martin's True Crime Library paperbacks are better than the most terrifying thriller, because it's all true! The next time you want a crackling good read, make sure it's got the St. Martin's True Crime Library logo on the spine—you'll be up all night!

Charles E. Spicer, Jr.
Senior Editor, St. Martin's True Crime Library

W9-BBY-051

At midnight on that windswept summer evening, the full moon shot daggers of gray light through the dense eucalyptus trees as the sturdy breeze continued its relentless path through the groves.

In the distance a group of young people were staggering through the overgrowth making their unsteady way toward the center of the eucalyptus jungle.

Suddenly, the only girl in the foursome fell to the ground wearily, her eyes drooping from the effects of the drugs she had been given a few minutes earlier. The boys looked down at the girl, barefoot and bedraggled. Then one of them grabbed a handful of her silky blond hair and pulled her further into the overgrowth. They said nothing. They knew what was coming next . . .

IN THE NAME OF
SATAN

WENSLEY CLARKSON

St. Martin's Paperbacks

IN THE NAME OF SATAN

Copyright © 1997 by Wensley Clarkson.

ISBN: 0-312-96389-0

Printed in the United States of America

St. Martin's Paperbacks edition/February 1998

10 9 8 7 6 5 4 3 2 1

Notes of Gratitude

The idea of using a leaden, dispassionate word like "acknowledgments" for this section cannot begin to express the depth of my feelings for the many individuals who have made this book possible. I owe them my deepest and most heartfelt gratitude.

First to my literary manager Peter Miller and my editor Charles Spicer. Without them this book would never have happened. Their support and guidance have been very much appreciated. Also, many, many thanks to Anthony Bowman. Then there is Frank Abatemarco, who first brought this case to my attention and whose investigative skills have proved so invaluable in helping me put this book together.

Then there are the townsfolk of Arroyo Grande and San Luis Obispo, California, who welcomed me with such enthusiasm and hospitality. They include: Robert Dyer, Bridgette Herrick, the offices of Judge Larry Reiner, the offices of Sheriff Ed Williams, Elyse Neilsen Walter and her family, Allan Hutkin, Carol Roberts of the *Telegram-Tribune*, and the staff of the Arroyo Grande Library. There are many others whose confidentiality I have respected, and therefore cannot thank by name.

But one of my biggest debts of gratitude must go to Tom Parsons, formerly of the *Five Cities Times Press Recorder*.

Also a special word of thanks to Elyse's good friends Shannon Plotner and Angel Katyryni. Without them this book would not have been possible.

Lastly, to Mark Sandelson and Alexis for providing all the usual facilities that have made this and so many of my other books possible.

There is now just a small glass jar with a photograph of a laughing, smiling Elyse Marie Pahler to indicate the position in the eucalyptus grove where she met her untimely death.

But the people of Arroyo Grande know precisely where it is. Among the teenagers at the high school, it is difficult to find anyone who did not know that Elyse met her dreadful end on the night of July 22, 1995.

There are doctors and nurses, storekeepers, bar boys, and cabdrivers who will never forget what happened that night. There are countless teenage girls and boys whose lives still reflect the trauma of that tragic event.

For every newsperson who was then in Arroyo Grande, the story of Elyse Pahler's murder stands as the biggest story they have ever covered. Every policeman who visited the site of her death marks her killing as the worst tragedy to which he has ever had to respond.

For Elyse Pahler was the ultimate victim of circumstance and tragedy in an ever worsening world whose moral ineptitude seems to know no boundaries.

Author's Note

Quotations from written material appear, with few exceptions, without the editorial "[sic]." When it seems that a word was inadvertently missing, it has been added for the sake of clarity. Mistakes in punctuation, grammar, and spelling have been corrected in certain instances, but in others it was felt that retaining an error helped convey the flavor of a document and the style of the person being quoted.

All the dialogue represented in this book was constructed from available documents, courtroom recollections, and the memories of participants.

Introduction

Everyone is capable of killing under some circumstances, but none of us kills under all circumstances. Killings occur only when certain people with certain learning experiences find themselves in certain situations.

The killing that is described in this book involves juvenile offenders. No one knows all the triggers that unleashed these killers into our midst. But whatever went into turning these three boys into youngsters who allegedly killed, it is possible that one or more of just a handful of known factors played a part: poverty, substance abuse, and a complete breakdown in understanding the difference between good and evil.

Sadly, very little is being done to reduce the prevalence of all these factors. The worst news is that, as a result, both the annual number and rate of juvenile homicides have been increasing, will continue to increase, and will probably reach record high proportions by the turn of the century.

Criminologists insist there is a link between poverty and crime among juveniles. Yet in the case you are about to read, no such problems existed. That's what makes it so disturbing. This is a crime that goes against the grain of popular opinion and provides a chilling reminder that violent death can cross social divides with great ease.

The presence of narcotics in the lives of these three young offenders simply provides the criminologists with something to blame. For there is no definite data on the number or percentage of homicides committed by youths under the influence of drugs. Although the most recent research suggests that as many as two-thirds of all juvenile killings are committed by youngsters high on drugs.

Drugs create confusion, lower inhibitions, impair judgment, and make youngsters more susceptible to peer influence. But whatever the role played by drugs in the crime featured here, drug abuse is clearly a factor that often increases the likelihood that a juvenile will kill.

The federal government estimates that casual drug abuse in the United States has decreased over the last five years but that frequent use of certain substances— most notably cocaine and its derivative, crack—has significantly increased over the same period. For example, between 1985 and 1988, federally sponsored household surveys found that the number of weekly cocaine users rose from 647,000 to 862,000 and the number of daily cocaine users rose from 246,000 to 292,000. During the same period, emergency room visits related to cocaine jumped from 8,000 to 46,000.

American society does little in the 1990s to try to stem the tide of juvenile crime, and as this case so clearly indicates, the problems that lie beneath the surface are virtually insurmountable.

We are all responsible, defiled, unhappy.
We have stolen with the burglar whose
face we do not know, we have murdered
with the parricide about whom we read
in the newspapers, raped with the lewd,
cursed with the blasphemous . . .

——Henry Troyat, *Firebrand: the Life*
of Dostoyevsky

Prologue

Heat, on the twenty-second of July in 1995, hung over the Californian community of Arroyo Grande like a laminated pall. Even after dusk had fallen, layers of smog and dust drifted across the mesa from the nearby city of San Luis Obispo and its sprawling complex of industrial plants, orchards, and mushrooming subdivisions.

Fog-freshened San Simeon, where William Randolph Hearst lived, might have been five thousand miles to the north instead of only fifty. To those living in their isolated homes on the Nipomo Mesa at the northeast edge of Arroyo Grande, the temperatures were intolerable.

By rights the deserted eucalyptus groves that dominated the area should have been cooler than they were with the easterly winds coming off the Pacific coast at nearby Grover Beach. But the breeze was filled with hot dusty air that stung on contact with bare skin.

At midnight on that windswept summer evening, the

full moon shot daggers of gray light through the dense eucalyptus trees as the sturdy breeze continued its relentless path through the groves.

In the distance a group of young people were staggering through the overgrowth guided by an erratic yellow flashlight waving from side to side as brittle twigs snapped underfoot. Gradually, they were making their unsteady way toward the center of the eucalyptus jungle.

Suddenly, the only girl in the foursome fell to the ground wearily, her eyes drooping from the effects of the drugs she had been given a few minutes earlier. For a moment complete silence overcame the group. The boys looked down at the girl, barefoot and bedraggled, and then joined her. She squinted into the beam of their flashlight as they began smoking pot.

A few minutes later she began crying. One of them swayed to his feet and peered down at her. Then he grabbed a handful of her silky blond hair and pulled her roughly to her feet. She cried from the pain as they dragged her farther into the overgrowth. They said nothing. They knew what was coming next.

They quickly found a clearing in the center of the eucalyptus grove. Two of the boys pushed the terrified girl back on the dusty ground. The other one removed the belt from his pants, slipped it over her neck, and pulled it taut. Her eyes bulged in terror as she desperately tried to breathe.

The older boy looked at his friend as the belt was squeezed tighter and tighter. It felt surreal. More vivid than a nightmare, but somehow it didn't feel as if it was really happening.

The young girl's body convulsed as the belt tightened its viselike grip. Then she went limp. The boy standing over her pulled the belt from her neck and took a long steel hunting knife out of its sheath.

The six-inch blade glinted menacingly in the moonlight. He plunged it into her neck. As she tried to fight back and clawed desperately at the belt, one of the others held her arms down to prevent her from struggling.

Then, in the hot, still night, there came a disturbing sound—a monotonous wail that continued without interruption. Whether the sound was a scream or a moan, or whether it came from a man or a woman, none of the residents tucked up in the nearby houses dotted across the Nipomo Mesa heard a thing.

The eerie wail went on, soaring over the whistling wind. But still no one heard it.

Just then, one of the youths pressed his hand hard over her mouth to quell the noise. She struggled. The strange, high-pitched sound was muffled, but it continued cascading through the hot night air. Then the pressure of his weight forced her head back onto the broken twigs as she bravely struggled and kicked.

The knife was passed to another one of the youths. They took turns stabbing her a total of twelve times. Over and over.

As she lay moaning on the ground, crying for her mother and praying to God, the boys stomped the back of her neck and dragged her by her feet farther into the eucalyptus grove, where she eventually bled to death.

Just a quarter of a mile away from that awful scene, David Pahler had just walked into his daughter Elyse's bedroom to say good night to her. He looked down at the bed and immediately realized she had artfully placed three pillows under the covers so it looked as if she was asleep.

David Pahler sighed. It was the third time in recent months that his pretty, blond fifteen-year-old daughter had sneaked out of the family's comfortable four-bedroom house on the Nipomo Mesa.

Pahler presumed that the phone call his daughter had received a few hours earlier must have been from the person she'd crept out to meet that bone-dry summer's night.

Pahler knew his daughter had experimented with alcohol and marijuana in the recent past. "We had even talked to her about sneaking out and about making good and bad choices," he later recalled.

But this time he had an even worse feeling than usual about where his daughter might have gone.

David Pahler swiftly headed out of the house to see if there was any sign of her in the vicinity. He checked the back and front yards. Then he walked back to his car in the driveway and began aimlessly driving around the dusty back roads and tracks that crisscrossed the Nipoma Mesa, near their home on the aptly named Hidden View Estate.

Elyse's last words to her parents before she disappeared earlier that night kept repeating in David Pahler's head:

"I love you and I'm going to bed."
"I love you and I'm going to bed."
"I love you and I'm going to bed."

One

Nothing much happened in Arroyo Grande until Wednesday, March 31, 1886, when bloodshed and violence came to this sleepy little backwater with a vengeance.

On that day a man was murdered, his wife was critically wounded, and a gang of self-styled vigilantes hung the suspects—a father and son—without benefit of a legitimate trial.

This remarkable outburst of violence—which became a slice of local Wild West history—had been sparked by a quarrel between neighbors over a parcel of land both claimed was their own.

But the most significant aspect of this horrendous sequence of events is that vigilante justice prevailed—and to this day there are many in Arroyo Grande who believe that every murderer should face a similar type of retribution.

The earliest inhabitants of Arroyo Grande were the northern Obispeno Chumash Indians, who still occupied the area at the time of contact with the first Spanish explorer, Juan Cabrillo.

When the Latins masterminded the colonial settlement of this part of California, the Arroyo Grande Valley was split into two major ranchos, which were granted by the Mexican government in 1840.

In the mid-1860s a severe drought decimated the cattle population, forcing the large ranchos to subdivide property and sell smaller parcels to new settlers for agricultural use.

In 1863 the San Luis Obispo County Board of Supervisors established the township of Arroyo Grande.

Today's Arroyo Grande—set in hilly terrain just southeast of San Luis Obispo—has a population of less than 20,000 and is a picturesque Californian town skirting busy Interstate 1 and Highway 101.

The city has four parks and an impressive twenty-six-acre sports complex with playing fields and tennis courts. The hiking trails along the Arroyo Grande Creek are considered among the finest in the state.

But the crime figures in Arroyo Grande tell a different story: One hundred violent crimes were reported by the townsfolk in 1995, which means inhabitants had a higher than average chance of becoming a violent crime statistic.

And throughout the county various infamous crimes have occurred over the previous few years.

The worst was when a man stuck a Magnum to the head of an airline pilot and made him nose-dive his aircraft into a mountain, wiping out thirty-eight crew and passengers.

It later emerged that the man had been angry at the boss of the airline, who'd fired him a few days earlier, so he'd shot him first in the aircraft and then headed for the cockpit.

On another occasion in 1983, six people were murdered in a drug-related mass homicide in a house in Pismo Beach.

"When people get murdered in this county, they seem to go out with a bang," says local journalist Robert Dyer.

But many of the law-and-order problems that existed specifically in Arroyo Grande centered around the town's teenagers.

Over the previous few years, there had actually been numerous gang-related crimes, including frequent shootings and stabbings.

As journalist Dyer pointed out, "This place has a large Latino population, and being a gangster is popular with many of these type of kids.

"The strange thing is that many of these gang members are from middle-class homes."

Gangs with names like the Aggies, Oceana 13, and Nipomo 13 openly paraded their membership at Arroyo Grande High School—the largest high school in the county.

Dyer explained, "There's a lot of peer pressure to join these gangs, but you don't just have to be a Latino to jump in. If you're a teenager in this town, you're either a jock, a gang member, or a homosexual—it's that simple."

Arroyo Grande was one of the so-called "five cities" in the south county, the others being Pismo Beach, Oceano, Grover Beach, and Shell Beach.

This meant that the 2,500 pupils at Arroyo Grande High came from all those cities plus the surrounding rural areas. Even with the majority of them traveling in by bus, trouble, it seemed, could not be avoided; and on one occasion a male student got on the school bus and began trying to stab various pupils. Thankfully, he was detained before he could inflict any really serious injuries, but the incident illustrated how danger lurked around every corner, even in an apparently quiet little backwater like Arroyo Grande.

Elyse Pahler, Shannon Plotner, and Angel Katyryni were three teenage girls, like millions of others, who have been drawn together by mutual interests and the promise of adventure.

Elyse, fifteen, was a very pretty, blond girl who lived in a nice house on the edge of Arroyo Grande, California. Her father was a hardworking construction worker, and her mother a fastidious homemaker. In her career plans Elyse leaned toward acting and singing, and she had a determined streak that seemed destined to make her an outstanding success.

Shannon Plotner, also fifteen and also blond and pretty, was the product of a broken home, but she'd managed, admirably, to retain a carefree attitude that endeared her to many. She worked hard at school and refused to let domestic discord get her down.

Angel Katyryni, fifteen, whose tall, slender, Slavic, dark-haired features complemented her two blond friends, admired her two friends' gutsy determination, but she was an altogether more laid-back person. However, she fully appreciated the bond of friendship between them.

These three had became really close friends after starting together as freshmen in the ninth grade at Arroyo Grande High School.

Elyse and Shannon always smiled warmly and were often mistaken for sisters. Together with Angel, they would turn the head of every young boy when they walked through the town on weekends. The girls often went down to Burger King or McDonalds for a coffee and to sneak a cigarette.

Shannon and Angel were fully aware that their pretty young friend Elyse was an extrovert party-type whose number one priority was to live life to the fullest. Sometimes they'd stand back and watch as carefree Elyse chatted to just about anyone who took her fancy.

"Elyse was really fun. She loved going out and was always telling us how she'd snucked out to see a boy or gone to a party," recalled Shannon.

In many ways the two other girls rather envied Elyse because she seemed so undaunted by the world and what lay ahead in her life. She was the eldest child in her family, yet didn't suffer the shyness that many oldest children do. Elyse also had an admirable ability to treat everyone as she found them. No inverted snobbery. No overcompetitiveness. Elyse was a relaxed, pretty teenager who only saw the good in everyone.

Elyse Marie "Cloie Moonshine" Pahler was born April 24, 1980, in Templeton, California, and had lived all her life in San Luis Obispo County. She attended elementary school in Templeton until 1989, when she and her mother Lisanne, father David, brother Ryan,

plus sisters Jenilee and Kristina moved to the Arroyo
Grande area of the Mesa.

Elyse was home taught by her mother during the sixth
and seventh grades, then she attended Paulding Middle
School and eventually Arroyo Grande High School,
where she'd just started her freshman year.

Elyse enjoyed school, got good grades, and was very
active in soccer, tennis, and theater. She was also a
member of the church choir and participated in a regular
Bible study class.

At the school campus, Elyse, Angel, and Shannon stuck
together most of the time even though virtually every
boy in their year had tried to persuade them to go out
on dates. They preferred the company of the older, more
mature boys in the classes above. "It wasn't that we
looked down on these kids in our year, we just didn't
rate many of them to talk to," Angel later explained.

A typical day as a freshman at Arroyo Grande High
started at around 7:30 A.M. when the three girls would
meet in the school yard and talk about boys, fashion,
makeup, and how annoying their parents were.

Class started at 7:55 A.M., following a roll call that
had become mandatory after a severe problem with ab-
sentee students. Two classes of fifty minutes each were
followed by a ten-minute break back in the school yard.
Then two more lessons would take the freshmen up to
lunch break from 12:05 to 12:45. Then it was back to
classes, which finished at 2:40 P.M.

As the biggest school in South County, Arroyo High
had its fair share of problems besides run-of-the-mill
class hopping. But during the girls' freshmen year, the

biggest scandal was when a boy stabbed another boy in the lunch hour after a furious row about a girl.

The town's chief of police Rick TerBorch turned up at the school within minutes of the alarm being raised, and the victim was rushed to a hospital, where he thankfully recovered from his injuries. His assailant was later given a youth-custody sentence.

But that incident set off alarm bells among the school staff, and Chief TerBorch agreed with the school governors to train up a special schools policeman to keep a permanent eye on proceedings at the 2,000-plus pupil establishment.

Elyse, Shannon, and Angel steered well clear of the troublemakers at school. The three friends supported each other by hanging out together virtually all the time. That way they could avoid being pulled into the wrong type of crowd. Or so they reckoned.

It also meant that when their Arroyo High class traveled down to the outskirts of Los Angeles to visit Magic Mountain on a school trip, the three close friends experienced all the scary rides together.

Elyse persuaded them to go on the huge roller coaster that dominated the skyline at the amusement park. Angel later recalled: "Elyse got off on the excitement of that ride. We found it terrifying. She loved it so much she wanted to go over and over again."

On the bus journey back home up Highway 101, Elyse and her friends got into tearful conversations about their favorite Californian rock star, Beck. Elyse had first been attracted to the singer and songwriter Beck Hansen when he emerged in 1994 with his single "Loser," an upbeat slab of post-grunge pop that earned him a major recording deal. Beck's album *Mellow Gold* was an unashamed reference to marijuana, something that Elyse and her friends had experimented with.

Elyse had photos of the handsome slacker Beck Hansen on the ceilings and walls of her large bedroom at home. She particularly adored his album *One Foot in the Grave*. Shannon and Angel teased her about her obsession with the morbid record because it seemed so out of character for their bubbly friend.

Elyse was fascinated by Beck Hansen's childhood, which was split between the colorful, artistic world of Los Angeles, where he lived with his mother Bobbe Hansen—whose Hollywood home became a hangout for punk bands—and the more parochial world of Kansas, where he spent the summers with his paternal grandfather, a Presbyterian preacher.

With Elyse it was the other way around. She adored trips to her eccentric, strong-willed grandmother Elyse Walter's ranch in Santa Ynez, where she'd take off on horseback for hours of riding. Elyse found life back in boring, sleepy Arroyo Grande rather unsatisfactory, and she insisted to her two best friends that she had big plans to break into show business when she left school.

"I'm going to make it. I know it," she proudly exclaimed as the three friends sat together at the back of the huge school bus as it drove back up to Arroyo Grande from that trip to Magic Mountain. The others rolled their eyes, but they had a sneaking suspicion that Elyse could get anything she wanted.

TWO

Rumbling like an angry god, the rusting red 1985 Toyota pickup cruised around the center of Arroyo Grande before easing into a prime spot right by the door to Burger King. The thudding sounds of death metal rock band Slayer blared from the truck's stereo system.

"Slice her flesh to shreds, watch the blood flow free."

Then Travis Williams switched off the ignition, and the music suddenly died.

The Arroyo High pupils who gathered weekends at the restaurant looked away as the four boys emerged from the truck and strolled toward the building.

Joe Fiorella, fourteen, Jacob Delashmutt, fifteen, Royce Casey, sixteen, and Travis Williams, seventeen, attracted more than their fair share of attention in the town—for all the wrong reasons.

Fiorella and Delashmutt attended the high school, while Williams had a fearsome reputation as a short-tempered tough guy.

After being kicked out of his own family home, Williams had been a guest at the home Fiorella shared with his mom, Betsy Leo, and his younger brother. They'd even vacationed together in Colorado the previous summer.

Royce Casey was the stranger in the pack. He attended the Lopez High School, also in Arroyo Grande, and seemed a much more levelheaded character than the others.

But all four youths' main claim to fame was that they played in their own rock band, Hatred, specializing in so-called death metal music, singing about Satan with gruesome regularity. The boys even wrote their own songs and splashed out a few hundred dollars to make one recording. They had 200 copies printed with the hope of selling to death metal fans in Arroyo Grande.

Those who heard Hatred said the music was sound-shatteringly loud with contrasting zing guitar and very loud drumbeats. It was hard to concentrate on, but the words were continually obsessed with the devil, satanism, and sacrificing virgins.

Young Joe Fiorella's mom, Betsy Leo, was a well-known figure in the town after being the subject of a story in the local *Telegram-Tribune* newspaper in July, 1980, just three weeks after Joe's birth. The article described her switch as a former abortion counselor who taught sex education at schools to the president of the now defunct Arroyo Grande chapter of the Pro-Family Forum, a branch of a pro-life national organization based in Texas. Probably about the most drastic turnaround anyone could have.

However, it was Leo's former involvement in the occult that caused much talk around town. Years before, the same article reported that Leo had delved into extrasensory perception, hypnotism, and astrology. Leo had become a licensed minister working with inmates at the county jail and the California Men's Colony. A falling-out with her church affiliate, the Central Foursquare Church of Arroyo Grande, led to her giving up the prison ministry.

Leo denied that she ever practiced satanism or witch-craft and prided herself on being open to both her sons about religion.

She forthrightly told one local newspaper reporter, "I have always valued life. I was a child of the sixties. We were kind and loving, and we were going to do things differently than our parents. Collectively, we have failed."

Fiorella, Delashmutt, Casey, and Williams' appearance at the Burger King that afternoon caused a ripple of interest because the four youths were rumored to be drinking heavily and doing drugs.

"They gave the impression they didn't give a fuck about anyone," recalled one of their associates. "It was like they'd walk into Burger King as if they were something real special. Like we'd all be impressed."

Joe Fiorella, the youngest of the group, was in the

habit of getting fixations for girls and following them around town in a creepy manner. He was the cold, silent type, and was into wearing extremely dirty, baggy, grungy clothes with long greasy hair and a fondness for torn tie-dyed sweatshirts similar to those worn in the boys' favorite movie, *River's Edge*, starring Keanu Reeves.

Joe played the drums with Hatred, the group the boys had formed. He was renowned for manically smashing his sticks down relentlessly during the band's rehearsals at his home on the nearby Nipomo Mesa.

Jacob Delashmutt was a much more talkative character with a neatly cut ponytail. The girls found him a little less creepy, but they kept their distance from him all the same. Like Joe, he favored the grunge look. "But at least he wore a clean shirt every day," commented one contemporary of the boys.

Delashmutt had a talent for art, and specialized in drawing weird monsters and death scenes that seemed to paint a disturbing picture of his subconscious. His parents were devout Mormons, and one brother was a missionary, the other a teacher. But that didn't seem to stop him being a law unto himself.

Delashmutt had a drug problem, and even attended the nearby Mariposa Community Recovery Center, where he encountered Elyse Pahler. Elyse was sent to the clinic for counseling after her parents had found a stash of cannabis in her room.

As one family friend of the Pahlers explained, "Elyse's use of cannabis was about the only contradiction in her character. It was a weakness, but then she was hardly the only bored kid in Arroyo Grande to experiment with soft drugs."

Jacob Delashmutt sat opposite Elyse as more than a dozen youngsters received group counseling at the center. His drug problems were far more serious—he was taking vast quantities of amphetamines and had started being absent regularly from school without explanation.

Elyse and Delashmutt did not exactly connect at these counseling sessions, but Delashmutt couldn't help noticing Elyse. However, there is absolutely no indication that she returned his attention in any way. He was intrigued by her happy smiling face, and started to wonder if he might be able to persuade her to be his friend.

Royce Casey, the quiet man of the group of four youths, looked altogether more civilized than the others, and had even been known to date the occasional girl from high school.

At the Burger King that day, none of the boys spoke to anyone else and sat in a corner sharing two chocolate milk shakes. One of them was avidly listening on a Walkman to the boys' favorite rock group, Slayer, whose lyrics also constantly referred to devil worship and suicide.

Two of the boys wore T-shirts featuring the group Suicidal Tendencies, another death metal outfit.

But the four youths were by no means the only schoolkids into groups like Slayer and Suicidal Tendencies at the time. Perhaps significantly, most of the girls at the school hated the scary lyrics that talked of death and the devil. "They thought death metal was kind of macho, but most of us reckoned it was pathetic," explained one girl who knew the youths.

And the youths were starting to get an altogether more

disturbing reputation for other things as well. One of Delashmutt's neighbors, Kara Herrick, later revealed, "We heard that Jacob and his friends were interested in real devil worship. They were strange boys. They kept to themselves and hardly spoke, but I could see there was something bad going on with them."

Gordon Milton, a religious historian at the University of California, in nearby Santa Barbara, spent thirty years studying unconventional religious groups, including satanism.

He found that perpetrators of violent crime involving satanism are usually white kids who live in middle-class suburban areas. "It's usually young teenagers who are most likely to pull something like this."

Milton claimed one of the appeals of teenage satanism was teenage sexual anxiety. "It's a teenage power trip. Young teenagers have awakened, but society says wait, so they're in an in-between stage."

Joe Fiorella, Jacob Delashmutt, Travis Williams, and Royce Casey were certainly looking for a "power trip." Perhaps it was only a matter of time before they found the perfect excuse.

Three

The screams were bloodcurdling. Ear-piercing yells. Long screeches that echoed into the darkness beyond.

Then silence. A couple of minutes of blissful silence. Then another scream. This time even more horrendous. Even more high-pitched. Even more agonizing.

Elyse Pahler and her two good friends Shannon Plotner and Angel Katyryni were sitting in their movie theater seats glued to the screen as Tom Cruise drank blood and caused mayhem in *Interview With the Vampire*. It was the fifth time they'd seen the movie in less than three weeks. They loved every minute gory detail, including being provoked into screaming fits with alarming regularity. That was part of the enjoyment of this particular movie.

Frequently other moviegoers would complain that the girls were disrupting their concentration with their gasps of "Oh, my God!" followed by yet another scream. The girls' would giggle in response and apologize but they loved being scared. They also loved Tom Cruise.

For this was a movie that even its normally whole-some star Cruise admitted was "a very erotic picture with lots of biting going on." He told one Hollywood scribe: "The hard part is learning to bite someone in a different way each time. Each kill has to tell the story of that relationship."

Elyse, Shannon, and Angel were pretty regular visi-tors to the movie theater at the end of Shannon's road in the center of Arroyo Grande because there wasn't much else to do in town. Sometimes they'd even watch back-to-back performances of a particularly good movie just for something to do. One of their other favorites was *Slackers*, about a group of young people managing to avoid all the usual responsibilities. Like millions of young Americans in 1994, they found it easy to relate to the movie.

However, spine chillers like *Interview With the Vam-pire* made the girls very wary of the weirder kids in town. Especially those who were into so-called death metal music, with all its satanic connotations. There were rumors at school that some pupils were practicing devil worship, and there had been talk of a couple of boys trying to snatch a young virgin off the streets of Arroyo Grande. Nobody took the stories that seriously, but the three girls pledged to keep away from the weirdos.

Like every teenage girl, all three acknowledged the need to be in their own crowd. They provided each other with friendship and support.

"We knew we'd be okay if we stuck together," re-called Shannon.

Being in a crowd also provided a checkup on their own thinking and help with schoolwork and confidential problems. And lots of social life.

Crowds also made contact with boys easier because they also projected a mass sexual image that was absolutely irresistible to boys. It was a much more potent appeal than one girl could summon on her own.

Elyse, Shannon, and Angel were a small crowd who had truly solidified. But sometimes the girls seemed so firmly knitted together that it made it hard for anyone else to join them.

Elyse brought out a scrapbook, and the three girls huddled around it. She showed Angel and Shannon a picture of herself as a small girl before the family moved to their home in Arroyo Grande. She remembered her early childhood as happy and content.

The three girls would regularly end up going back to the Pahler house and gossiping in Elyse's bedroom until the early hours.

While her parents and brother and sisters sat at the other end of the house watching TV, she and her friends would chat on about school and boys. They had come to the conclusion that school was a difficult place to learn. With 2,500 pupils, Arroyo Grande High School was indeed a crowded place.

Also the dropout rate was soaring every year, and the girls sometimes found it very difficult to avoid being sucked into the war zone that existed at school.

"Guys were often hassling us, trying to get us to agree to dates. But we told the ones we didn't like to get lost," recalled Angel.

"That's why we liked it so much at Elyse's place. We could relax, chill out, talk about everything we wanted without being hassled."

Elyse's brightly colored room featured collages of her own Mona Lisa–type paintings. She had bunk beds in the corner even though she didn't share the room with any of her brothers or sisters. There was also a couch by the French doors that led into the backyard, plus a big fluffy chair covered in pillows.

On the dressing table were hundreds of pills in bottles piled high. "There were bottles everywhere," recalled Shannon. "Elyse couldn't stand taking any pills, so she kept them instead."

The sizable Pahler house had been personally constructed by Elyse's dad David under close scrutiny from his wife Lisanne. It was a peach-colored detached four-bedroom dwelling with a long curved driveway up to the house from a lane that ran onto the next nearest house one hundred yards away. Beyond that were the desolate eucalyptus groves that covered the nearby hilly terrain.

"It was the sort of house you wouldn't want to be in on your own," explained Angel. "The only thing you could see out of Elyse's French doors was a big hill with trees and things. I remember those trees were always rustling in the wind. I reckon Elyse often asked us back to her place because she didn't much like being in that room on her own at night, as it was at the opposite end of the house from the rest of the family."

Elyse's favorite game was to jump off the roof of the garage onto a trampoline in the yard. Some days she'd do it for hours while all sorts of adolescent thoughts raced through her mind. She also found it a good place to retreat after a row with her mom and dad.

Not surprisingly, as those teenage thoughts kicked in, Elyse became increasingly frustrated by her life. She adored her two best friends Shannon and Angel, but she wanted to explore certain boundaries quicker than her contemporaries. She had this unquestionable adventurous spirit, and it couldn't be contained much longer.

And the isolated position of her bedroom at the other end of her family's house was to prove very relevant to the continuing adventures of Elyse Pahler.

In late 1994 she started getting into the habit of sneaking out through the French doors from her bedroom and meeting boys or hanging out at local parties.

This then rapidly developed into something even more daring, as Angel later explained: "Elyse started having boys in her room. She could get them in and out of the house without her parents knowing. She loved taking those sort of risks."

Angel and Shannon never forgot how one time they were all holed up in Elyse's room. She was bored and suggested that she call up a boy she knew and demand that he drive around, pick them all up, and take them dancing. The other two—all of them were just fourteen years old at the time—were shocked that Elyse had an older boy on tap and was prepared to skip out of the house without telling her parents.

Angel and Shannon refused to go out with Elyse's male friend that night because they didn't know him, so she went out with him alone. "She didn't seem worried. She was crazy, carefree," Shannon later recalled. "We just wouldn't take the same sort of risks as Elyse."

Elyse's parents had only the vaguest idea that she was sneaking out of the house, because Elyse's room was strictly out-of-bounds to her mom and dad. It had become virtually a self-contained apartment for the pretty teenager.

It wasn't as if David and Lisanne Pahler didn't care what their daughter was doing. They just didn't want to have nonstop confrontations with Elyse. They thought, understandably, it would be better to treat her with a soft approach instead of shouting and screaming at her and alienating her as so many families seemed to do.

Soon Elyse's adventures around Arroyo Grande became the main topic of conversations when the three girls were together either in the school yard or back at her house off Chamisal Road. She told her friends she'd tried most drugs "more than just a few times." Elyse had even been expelled for five days in junior high for drinking alcohol.

"I guess we kinda envied Elyse. She seemed to be havin' a good time all the time. We loved hearing about her romances and all the people she came across," remembers Angel to this day.

Elyse encouraged her two close friends to get out and about more. "She wanted us to stick together more," recalls Angel.

The other two tried to stick closer to their good friend, but they just weren't prepared to take the same kind of risks. Explained Shannon, "It was always fun with Elyse, but we couldn't handle it as well as her."

Naturally, these three adolescent girls spent much of their time analyzing and reanalyzing the boys at their school and around Arroyo Grande. They even devised a league table of the top thirty boys they'd come across, regularly swooning in the process.

But they also made up a list of the ones they'd least like to meet in a dark alleyway.

Among those on the list were fifteen-year-old Jacob Delashmutt and fourteen-year-old Joe Fiorella. Elyse's encounters with Delashmutt in the high school art class and at drug rehab counseling sessions had made her a bit wary of the youth. She was also disturbed by his attempts at painting devil figures and satanistic signs.

"They're real creepy pictures, and he is a complete weirdo," Elyse told her friends.

Then there was Joe Fiorella; he'd been expelled from the high school earlier that year and sent to the Community School in San Luis Obispo, only to be allowed back into the high school in the fall of 1994.

All three girls had noticed that Fiorella and Delashmutt hung around together, and sometimes they'd seen them staring in their direction during break time in the school yard. But then many adolescent boys tended to look longingly toward Elyse, Angel, and Shannon, so they took little notice.

Four

To numb themselves from the boredom of life in Arroyo Grande, Joe Fiorella, Travis Williams, Jacob Delashmutt, and their friend Royce Casey sniffed glue, got high on speed—anything to make themselves feel better.

They also regularly watched a 1986 movie called *River's Edge* starring the then little-known Keanu Reeves and veteran Hollywood star Dennis Hopper. The film centered around a high school kid in small-town America who murders his girlfriend and then finds his friends wondering what action they should take.

"It was a really cool movie, and we all talked about it in class many times," one of the boys' classmates at Arroyo Grande High later explained.

River's Edge was described by the *New York Times* as "[a] brilliant messy little picture . . . another triumph for the independent film movement . . . should cause people to argue and celebrate for years."

Delashmutt, Fiorella, Casey, and Williams certainly argued and celebrated *River's Edge*. They also became virtually addicted to the movie, even getting into the habit of quoting back dialogue from it in almost reverential terms.

One of their favorite lines came when the boy who killed the girl says:

> *"I get in a fight I go fucking crazy. Everything goes black and I fucking explode, like it's the end of the world. Who cares if this guy wastes me because I'm gonna waste him first."*

Delashmutt, Fiorella, Casey, and Williams would often watch *River's Edge* as they sat puffing on cannabis just like the characters in the film.

But the majority of their awe was reserved for a disturbing speech given by the kids' teacher when he discovered that most of his class had been shielding a murderer:

> *"No one in this class gives a damn that she's dead. It gives us a chance to feel superior and point out the fundamental moral breakdown in society. But it doesn't really affect us, does it? Because if it did, none of us would be in this classroom right now. We'd be out on the streets half crazy from a lack of sleep hunting down the killer with a gun."*

The other significant aspect of *River's Edge* was that it featured music by the boys' favorite death metal band, Slayer, including tracks called "Tormentor," "Evil Has No Boundaries," and "Die by the Sword."

The four boys were already particularly interested in this disturbing type of music. They believed groups like Slayer and Suicidal Tendencies were performing the best music in the land.

The violence-drenched lyrics of their favorite death metal groups had become a part of their everyday language. At high school those who encountered the two boys were struck by the way they spoke in a weird kind of ''death-speak.''

''They'd say things like 'cool sacrifice' or describe a pretty girl as a 'Satan witch.' It was as if they were speaking the words of the Slayer songs in normal conversation. It was difficult to get any real sense out of them,'' explained one fellow high school pupil.

The four boys were becoming sucked into their own world of death metal and satanism. Mundane activities like school, sports, and movies no longer mattered. Their agenda was veering away from the rest of their contemporaries.

At night Delashmutt and Casey would call around at Fiorella's house and end up staying up half the evening with Fiorella and his live-in best friend Travis Williams discussing Satan and listening to bands like Slayer.

The promotional material that came with the group's *Divine Intervention* CD included a collage of photographs depicting people who had died for Satan. Another photo showed a young man with the word Slayer carved on his arms with blood running from the wounds.

One of their favorites was the group's 1985 album entitled *Hell Awaits*. One song from the album, ''Necrophiliac,'' included the following lyrics:

*"Virgin child now drained of life, your soul cannot
be free."*

The boys were entranced by these lyrics and sang
them over and over again. Then they'd discuss them in
intricate detail before concluding that such groups were
incredibly cool.

Bands like Slayer also inspired the boys to pledge that
their recently formed death metal group Hatred should
only glorify Satan in song.

The subject of finding a girl to sacrifice came up on
numerous occasions.

The idea was growing every time they discussed it.
And somehow the lyrics in those songs and their curiosity about satanism made it all begin to sound extremely interesting.

Fiorella, Delashmutt, and Casey also discovered during
the early winter months of 1994 that every aspect of the
ever-more bizarre human experience had a home on the
Internet.

The boys' growing interest in the occult was also informed by Joe Fiorella's growing library on the subject.
He was said to have enough books on the subject to line
one wall of his black-painted bedroom at home in Arroyo Grande.

He also had copies of pamphlets by satanists such as
the notorious Aleister Crowley. In it the author described
a ritual in which a toad was crucified after being kept
all night in an ark or chest. It was renowned as a factual
description of a ceremony he had devised and performed
several times himself.

The toad ended up being stabbed in the heart with a dagger as the participant says: "Into my hands I receive thy spirit." The animal was then cooked and eaten as a sacrament. Joe Fiorella was fascinated by this.

With access to the World Wide Web, Fiorella and his friends were soon dialing up "Hell, The Online Guide to Satanism," "Altar of the Unholies," "Satan's Playground," and more than a dozen other sources of information about the netherworld and those fascinated by it.

The Church of Satan offered membership information. For a onetime $100 fee, Fiorella and Delashmutt got an "impressively embossed" crimson membership card and a questionnaire to fill out and return. Their answers were then reviewed, and they were given full access to the entire, disturbing subject.

The boys also tried to enroll with Maledicta, a publishing company with a West Virginia address, who offered dozens of titles on black magic, the occult, satanic rituals, and other aspects of devil worship. Its home page featured a large picture of a half-naked woman bound in rope.

Maledicta's Church of Satan opened on page one with this quote from satanist author and devil worshiper Anton LaVey:

"With heart and hand I pledge you while I load my gun again, you will never be forgotten or the enemy forgiven, my good comrade . . ."

The two boys sent off for books such as LaVey's *The Satanic Rituals*. "Learn how to perform the Black Mass,

the Call to Cthulhu, Satanic Baptisms and much more,''
promised the cover blurb.

Fiorella and Delashmutt were said to become enrap-
tured by the information that was flowing across their
computer screens, including personal ads—''SWF en-
joys sacrifice, mutilation . . .''—and gruesome-looking
knives that could be ordered by mail.

Maledicta's sales pitch sounded bizarre:

''Maledicta is pleased to bring you a collection of
knives that will make any ritual a truly diabolical event!
Each knife is made of high carbon steel and handcrafted
in India by the government contractor for military
knives.

''Note: We in no way condone illegal activity, and it
is your responsibility to check local laws and regulations
before ordering knives. You must be eighteen years or
older to purchase items on this page.''

Much of the chat on the Internet consisted of sarcastic
attacks on Christianity and the obligatory responses by
Christian defenders. Some of the discussions under way
included ''Is it OK with God if I am gay?'' and ''Jesus
a GOOD man? HAHA, yeah right.''

While the topic of human sacrifices did not on the
surface seem to be overtly glorified on the Internet, it
was subtly mentioned with alarming frequency by regular long-winded attempts to dispel concerns about ritual
abuse.

The ''myth'' is perpetuated, they claim, by a few authors, psychologists, and police officers who use the subject to promote themselves and their projects.

One of the most lengthy reviews of ritual abuse is
presented by the Ontario Center of Religious Tolerance.
They cited a number of studies purporting to show the

incidence of ritual abuse was vastly exaggerated.

"All ritual abuse is criminal; most victimizes children; none is done in public. Thus, there are no accurate estimates of its incidence in society," they concluded.

Those who regularly chatted on the Internet with other so-called satanists would be asked to describe in vivid detail how a virgin had been sacrificed.

Fiorella and Delashmutt were undoubtedly intrigued and devised entire fantasies to recall to their fellow Internet satanists. As their obsession grew, so did their perspective on reality. This was fast becoming the only world they knew and enjoyed. Sometimes they felt as if they really had sacrificed a virgin. They also started to wonder if they should try it for real.

But it is clear the two youths didn't appreciate the difference between fantasy and reality. Those two worlds were about to meet head-on in a destructive collision course. They wanted to devour every piece of information that might help them to gain the ultimate "ticket to hell."

Five

On the dusty, windswept mesa less than a mile behind Elyse Pahler's house was a vast redundant water pipe on twenty-foot legs—it overshadowed the area like some sort of prehistoric dinosaur.

The rusting hulk of metal was open at both ends, and no one quite knew why it was still standing. It had evolved over the years into a teenager's playground where bored youths congregated away from their parents' watchful eye, and was called the "Pipe of Death."

It was here on numerous warm spring days in 1995 that Jacob Delashmutt, Joe Fiorella, Travis Williams, and their friend Royce Casey would retreat from all the restrictions and law-abiding codes of Arroyo Grande.

The boys frequently tried to persuade girls at Arroyo Grande High to join them at the Pipe of Death, but the promise of ''havin' fun'' usually meant a cocktail of illicit drugs, and most girls found that idea a complete turnoff.

To enter the pipe, the youths scrambled up the ladder attached to its legs and then settled together in the center, lit up some crank, and talked about their growing interest in satanism. They'd often shout at the top of their voices and listen to the echoes reverberating through the walls of the pipe. They liked the feeling that no one in authority was anywhere near them. They could do what the hell they liked.

Sometimes, the boys would dare each other to walk along the top of the pipe, precariously balanced like trapeze artists with their arms outstretched. The pipe earned its gruesome nickname about ten years earlier when a boy fell from it and broke his back. He actually survived, but the Arroyo Grande High School rumor mill twisted the story to the point where everyone thought the boy had in fact died.

That pipe represented yet another escape from reality for Delashmutt, Fiorella, Casey, and Williams. They had grown bored of trying to find something to do in the center of Arroyo Grande. In their eyes, they had been left with no choice but to find a secretive bolt-hole and start doing drugs to drown out the tedium of their lives.

Besides crank, the boys had grown particularly fond of amphetamines. They enjoyed the hypertension that came with "speed," and found that the drug made them alert and active—unlike crank, which slowed them down and made them less capable of reaching decisions.

Being decisive was a very big problem for Delashmutt, Fiorella, Casey, and Williams. They had spent much of their teens drifting around school and drifting around town. Fiorella only started to truly focus in on the occult when he realized that his pals were keen to get involved. Eventually, his superior knowledge of the subject matter meant that, despite being the youngest in the group, he could be their leader. It was the first time in his short life that he'd ever felt any responsibility for anything, and he enjoyed the feeling.

Up there in the Pipe of Death, Fiorella would often bring one or two of his devil worshiping books and enthrall the others by reading out excerpts. They would switch on their ghetto blaster and play Slayer or Suicidal Tendencies at full volume while the crank and speed kicked in.

Inevitably, word began to filter around Arroyo Grande that the four boys were getting increasingly wrapped up in the drug scene, and everyone knew they spent much of their time in the Pipe of Death. The boys themselves were frequently conspicuous in their absence from school, and it eventually became a forgone conclusion that if they weren't in town, they were at the pipe.

"That pipe became their only means of escape. They could get blasted out of their brains in drugs and forget about the rest of the world," explained one school friend of Casey's.

As the brisk, swirling mesa winds turned warmer during the early part of 1995, the boys' interests became more and more focused on just one thing—satanism.

One warm spring day in March, 1995, Elyse Pahler and Angel Katyryni were walking home to Elyse's house from the bus stop when they noticed some of the older boys from Arroyo Grande High walking toward them on the street.

"Oh, no. Look the other way. It's the dweebs. Oh, my God," exclaimed Angel to her friend Elyse.

The two girls giggled nervously and realized they could not avoid passing Jacob Delashmutt, Joe Fiorella, Royce Casey, and Travis Williams.

As the boys got closer and closer, the two girls became aware that all four of them were staring intently in their direction.

Angel and Elyse looked down at the sidewalk in the hope they would pass without comment. Just then Elyse glanced up for a split second only to find herself looking directly into the watery eyes of Jacob Delashmutt.

"Hi. What're you doin'?" said the boy.

Neither girl answered at first. Instead an awkward, adolescent silence followed.

"Hey, don't you say 'Hi' to your seniors?" added Delashmutt cockily.

Both girls smiled hesitantly.

"Hi."

They looked back down at the sidewalk almost the instant they'd mouthed their reluctant greeting.

The other three egged on Delashmutt. One of them muttered something to him as the group of teenagers stood their ground awkwardly.

"So, what you doin'?"

Angel and Elyse shrugged their shoulders.

"We gotta get to Elyse's place to do our studies."

A chorus followed. "Ooooh. Got to get to Elyse's place to do your studies. Wow. You girls are serious."

Angel and Elyse didn't reply, but started walking. They then became aware of an air of tension suddenly hitting the proceedings.

"You gotta problem with us?" asked Delashmutt aggressively.

Angel registered the anger in his voice. She also smelled the pungent aroma of alcohol on his breath as it wafted in her direction. She stopped and turned.

"Problem? No. Why? Should we have a problem with you?"

Delashmutt smiled greasily.

"Why don't you two come over to my house, and we'll have ourselves a party?"

"No way," came Angel's quick-fire reply. She wanted to get the first words in because she feared that Elyse might seriously contemplate such an offer.

Delashmutt turned to Elyse, sensing her uncertainty.

"What about you? Why don't you come?"

Angel grabbed Elyse by the arm and pulled her around, and they walked off without another word.

Angel never forgot how much the boys had been swaying throughout the brief conversion.

"They were outta their heads on drugs and drink, and there was no way I'd go to their house," she later explained.

But what also stuck in Angel's mind was that she felt as if Delashmutt had been rehearsing his words before he approached them. She also noted that although Delashmutt did the talking, it was Joe Fiorella who seemed in charge.

Angel recalled, "It was like they'd planned it beforehand. Like they had an agenda. It was really weird. And I'm certain Joe Fiorella was calling the shots."

Not long after this incident, Elyse was looking out of the window of her bedroom when she noticed a figure on a push-bike across the deserted street outside her home.

On closer examination she realized it was Joe Fiorella. When he saw Elyse he smiled. She smiled back and closed the drapes. It seemed strange that he was hanging about outside, but she didn't really give it another thought.

Over the following few weeks, Elyse noticed Fiorella on numerous occasions loitering at exactly the same spot she had seen him originally. "It was as if he was keeping an eye on her," her friend Shannon later recalled.

But at that stage Elyse wasn't worried by the attention from Joe. "She thought he kinda liked her," added Shannon. "And Elyse wasn't the type to shy away from anyone."

Once again, Elyse's happy-go-lucky attitude meant that she never thought badly of anyone. If Joe Fiorella wanted to hang about outside her house day and night, that was kinda sweet. She'd even talk to him if he plucked up the courage to approach her.

At home Elyse continued to dominate proceedings with her bright and bubbly personality. Her parents were well aware that she had always been a strong individualist. She had no fear of meeting or talking with people, but she always tried to be helpful.

Even when they insisted she go to drug rehab, it didn't cause a big split in the family. Elyse knew she shouldn't get too involved with drugs and appreciated her parents' concern for her well-being. But that wouldn't dampen her natural curiosity.

Elyse clearly adored her family, but she was an independent, free spirit.

That Father's Day, Elyse wrote a loving poem to her

father, telling him that she loved him "every single day, every single hour." It was a poem truly written from the heart. Later her family recollected that it perfectly reflected the relationship that existed between father and daughter.

"For all her spirit of adventure, Elyse was a good, caring daughter. Nothing could take that away from her," Elyse's grandmother later explained.

Six

Despite those earlier brushes with them, Elyse Pahler was intrigued by what she kept hearing about Delashmutt, Casey, Fiorella, and Williams. She knew they were not regular types by any means, but every time Joe Fiorella turned up outside her house, she got quite a buzz out of knowing that he was there.

Angel and Shannon warned their close friend Elyse off the boys, and at first Elyse seemed to take notice of their advice. But as the summer of 1995 began, Elyse found herself growing increasingly restless about her life at home and school.

That spirit of adventure was far from dampened, and a vein of irresponsibility ran through Elyse. Nothing was going to change that—not even a very disturbing incident that occurred in May, 1995.

* * *

Elyse was in her customary good mood as she walked down the street toward her house after being dropped off by the high school bus one afternoon. She was doing extremely well in school, the term was soon to end, and she was looking forward to a summer vacation with her family and a trip up to her grandmother's ranch in Santa Ynez.

Even when her parents announced they intended to move to San Luis Obispo later that summer, she wasn't upset because she actually felt a change of scenery might be a good thing. In any case, she liked meeting new friends, climbing new challenges.

As Elyse turned the corner onto her street that afternoon, she noticed those four familiar boys, including Fiorella and Delashmutt, shouting and waving in her direction.

"Quick. You gotta help," yelled Jacob Delashmutt.

Elyse looked puzzled. The boys were pointing to the bottom of a bank at the side of the road that ran down to a eucalyptus grove. She couldn't understand what all the fuss was about.

"We gotta problem. Can you help?" shouted another of the boys.

Elyse approached hurriedly.

"There's a guy stuck down there. He's broken his leg. We gotta help him."

As Elyse got to the side of the bank, she found herself immediately surrounded by the four boys.

She turned around and saw the glint in their eyes. They were smiling really weirdly. What was going on? She was about to speak when a hand pushed her off balance.

Elyse fell and then rolled down the dusty bank. As she came to a halt, she became aware of another familiar voice in the distance.

"Hey. What're you boys doin'?"

The foursome at the top of bank scattered the moment they realized that Elyse's mom Lisanne was fast approaching.

Elyse dusted herself off and scrambled back up the side of the bank.

"You okay, honey?" her mother asked her.

"Sure," replied Elyse. She was puzzled and bemused by what had just happened. None of it seemed to make any sense. They pushed her down a bank after pretending there was someone down there. Why?

That night Elyse told her parents that she thought the boys might have been stalking her for a few days. But she insisted it was nothing serious. "They're just stupid, mixed-up kids. They won't do anything bad," she said.

As Elyse's grandmother later explained, "David and Lisanne did not think anything about it. You know what kids are like."

In any case, Elyse's attitude was so matter-of-fact that her parents decided there could not be any harm in what the boys were doing. She certainly wasn't worried by the boys' actions.

But she did later admit to her best friend Angel: "What happened was kinda weird. I just don't know why they did it."

Angel was just as mystified as her friend, but she instinctively knew that those boys were troublemakers. Elyse had even told her that Delashmutt and Fiorella had gotten more and more creepy toward her at school, as well.

"Just keep well away from them, Elyse," Angel said. Elyse just giggled nervously.

Angel wished she could convince her best friend of just how dangerous those boys were.

"In some ways Elyse was freaked out by those boys, but she was also very curious about them because they were so different from most of the boys we came across. I knew she wouldn't keep away from them like I told her," recalled Angel.

A few weeks later, at the end of that term, Elyse got good grades from her freshman year at Arroyo Grande High School and announced to her friends that she intended to get a job working at a theater in the nearby city of Oceano for the summer.

But on July 21, 1995, Elyse met Joe Fiorella, Jacob Delashmutt, Royce Casey, and Travis Williams at a friend's house. Neither Angel or Shannon were present that day.

Elyse got talking to Jacob Delashmutt and decided that they weren't so bad after all. She even confided to Delashmutt that her friends had warned her off them. Delashmutt laughed and assured the pretty blond teenager that they were all decent guys.

Across the room Joe Fiorella struck his familiar pose: quiet, eyes staring, mind turning over and over. But Elyse chose to ignore any misgivings she had felt before that day.

So when Jacob Delashmutt asked Elyse for her phone number, she saw no harm in giving it. In any case, the boys said they'd be getting hold of some "wicked weed," which she might like to try.

"Definitely," exclaimed Elyse, whose curiosity about

such things as marijuana never dampened.

Next morning, a breathless and excited Elyse called up her best friend Angel and told her all about her encounter with Delashmutt, Fiorella, Williams, and Casey the previous day.

"They're not so bad. I think you got them wrong," she told Angel.

"Just be real careful of them," replied Angel.

"Angel, I told you. They're cool."

"They're creeps, and you better watch out for them."

"I kinda like that Jacob . . ."

Angel broke in, "You're kidding me?"

"Nope. I think he's cute."

"He's a weirdo, Elyse."

"I gave him my phone number."

"Be careful, Elyse. Be very careful," said Angel.

"You worry too much, Angel. I might even see him tonight if I feel like it."

That night Delashmutt and Fiorella made a phone call to Elyse Pahler from the only public telephone at the Mesa View Market, just near her home. They told Elyse they had some marijuana and LSD to give her and arranged to meet at the end of her street.

While the other two were on the phone with Elyse, Royce Casey happened to walk into the market with a girlfriend. Delashmutt was later alleged to have told the older youth, "You won't want to miss this."

It is reported that Casey responded immediately. He knew precisely what Delashmutt meant.

Minutes later Delashmutt, Fiorella, and Casey moved off together toward the Pahlers' home.

As arranged, Elyse then slipped out of the house. She was wearing black sweatpants and a sweater over a thermal top, but no shoes.

The foursome walked less than a mile to a eucalyptus grove on Chamisal Lane. As they sat talking and smoking marijuana, Delashmutt allegedly walked behind Elyse, removed his belt, and looped it around the girl's neck with his arms crossed. He then quickly pulled it tight.

They had used the belt to try and prevent her from screaming. Fiorella then pulled a hunting knife from a sheath and began stabbing Elyse Pahler in the neck.

She tried to fight back and clawed desperately at the belt. Royce Casey then held her arms down to prevent her from struggling.

Delashmutt allegedly took over the stabbing after Fiorella had thrust his knife into her neck at least five times. Delashmutt stabbed Elyse in the back. He then handed the knife to Casey, who made two or three thrusts through her sweater and underwear.

Elyse Pahler cried out for her mother. Then she was stomped on by the boys. She prayed out loud to God and continued to cry for her mother's help. But it was too late.

Then they dragged her punctured body over to a tree and propped it up against a huge broken branch that lay across the ground.

Elyse Pahler bled to death within minutes.

Seven

On July 22, 1995, Shannon Plotner was awoken from a lazy Saturday morning lie-in by a phone call from Elyse's worried father David Pahler.

"Do you know where Elyse went last night?" he asked Shannon.

Shannon—still half asleep—tried to think straight.

"Why?"

"We have to know, Shannon. It's very important. Elyse never came home last night."

"Right." Shannon hesitated. She felt torn between wanting to make sure her good friend Elyse was safe and well—and not getting her in trouble with her parents.

"Do you know where she went?" asked an increasingly impatient David Pahler.

"No," answered Shannon truthfully. "I have absolutely no idea."

The line went dead.

Unfortunately, Elyse's other great friend Angel was not in when the Pahlers called her home. At first they wondered if Elyse and Angel were out together, but they soon established that Angel had gone to Stockton to visit her grandmother for the weekend. The Pahlers were growing very worried about their daughter's fate.

They were perfectly aware that she had snuck out on previous occasions, but she'd never been out the entire night.

Just a couple of hours after that first call to Shannon, the Pahlers rang her back to try and find out more clues about where their beloved daughter might have gone.

"I didn't have any ideas, so I wasn't much help. I felt so sorry for them. They were so desperate," recalled Shannon.

She then picked up the phone that morning and began calling her friends to find out if any of them knew where Elyse might be.

One girl told Shannon that a twenty-year-old youth who was a neighbor of Elyse's had left home a week earlier. "We thought maybe she'd run off with him," recalled Shannon.

With that possibility in mind, Shannon became convinced that her friend would eventually come home.

"I wasn't too freaked by Elyse going. I reckoned she'd be back by that evening. Nothing was going to happen to Elyse. She'd be fine. I was sure of that," Shannon later recalled.

That same Saturday morning, Elyse's worried parents David and Lisanne made contact with Arroyo Grande

Police Chief Rick TerBorch to report their daughter's disappearance.

Chief TerBorch listened patiently to Mr. and Mrs. Pahler, took down all the details, and then referred it as a missing person's case to San Luis Obispo County Sheriff Ed Williams, whose larger facilities would enable them to spread the net in an effort to locate Elyse as quickly as possible.

Williams—a safe, solid, dependable character with almost forty years' experience as a police officer—had handled hundreds of missing teenager cases and presumed, like many others at the time, that Elyse would probably show up within a matter of hours, or days. Boyfriends or arguments with parents were the most likely reason for her disappearance.

Sheriff Williams was renowned for his conservative outlook on life. He'd previously been police chief in Pismo Beach. Before that he'd been a cop in Los Angeles, 195 miles south, and had even been wounded in the line of duty. It was an injury that left him with a troublesome arm, but thankfully little else.

San Luis Obispo County—with its rolling hills, endless seascapes, and outstanding lakes—was a prime tourist destination. But as the sheriff would happily point out to anyone who would listen, "Let us not be lulled by its beauty into forgetting about our safety. This county has murders, rapes, robberies, and a narcotics problem, just like any other community in our country."

As sheriff, coroner, and marshal of the county, Williams was the controlling influence over any investigation launched in Arroyo Grande or any of the other cities in the area. He prided himself on his organizational skills and his undoubted ability to keep his departments well within their budgets.

He took a personal interest in setting up various call lines with an extensive information outlet through the Internet, where he proudly offered files on the department's organizational structure, crime stoppers online, wanted persons, child molesters ID line, and even a suggestion box for citizens not happy with the service he was providing.

Williams also encouraged the creation of a school resources officer at the Arroyo Grande High School, following increased criminal activity at the school.

But on that Saturday morning, the police did not respond quickly enough to the Pahlers' desperate plea for help in finding their missing daughter. They promised to get the local newspaper to run an article and photograph of Elyse. But they made it clear that while they fully sympathized with the family, there was little or nothing they could do other than hope Elyse got in contact.

By the following day—Sunday—the Pahlers became even more distraught about their missing daughter. They called Shannon Plotner and pleaded with her to try and recall who Elyse had been hanging out with in recent weeks in order to try and locate someone who might have been with her that previous Friday evening.

Shannon insisted she had no ideas, but was so worried because her friend hadn't come home as she'd predicted that she went around to the Pahler house to try and help them find their daughter.

Over that first weekend of Elyse's disappearance, no one even contacted Angel and asked her those same, all important questions that might have thrown up some vital clues. She remained at her grandmother's home in

Stockton completely unaware of what had happened to her best friend.

Meanwhile Shannon Plotner found her visit to the Pahler home a very heartbreaking experience. "They were just so upset, and it seemed as if no one could actually come up with any clues as to where Elyse might have gone."

Within forty-eight hours of her disappearance, the police received an unconfirmed report that Elyse had been seen with a man in Pismo Beach, just ten miles from Arroyo Grande. The caller—one of Elyse's classmates at Arroyo Grande High—insisted the blonde teenager had cut her hair and was living with the man, who was in his early twenties.

Perhaps rather hastily, the police decided that the claim had the ring of truth about it and passed it on to Elyse's parents. The Pahlers were far from convinced and insisted that when the local newspaper ran a missing person's report, they wanted their home phone number in the article to make sure that no one was afraid of coming forward with new information.

The small article and picture, which appeared on page two of the *Five Cities Times Press Recorder* ten days after Elyse's disappearance, stated:

ARROYO GRANDE—*Sheriff's detectives are asking for help in locating Elyse Marie Pahler, age fifteen, of Arroyo Grande.*

The missing teenager is described as five feet, seven inches tall, weighing 135 pounds, with blond hair and blue eyes. She was last seen on Saturday,

*July 22, in the Pismo Beach area, investigators
said.*

*Anyone with information is asked to call the
sheriff's detective bureau at 781-4500 or the girl's
parents at 489-5858.*

The Pahlers' close family and friends were surprised
by the tone of the article because it was clear the police
believed that Elyse was in the Pismo Beach area. They
felt that this suggested she had run away of her own
accord, and there was a definite lack of urgency about
the appeal.

The situation wasn't helped by some of Elyse's school
friends coming forward and clearly stating that the fifteen-year-old was a party girl who had probably run off
with some guy she met recently.

No one knows who or what provoked those calls.
Whether they were genuine mistaken sightings or
planned by someone to mislead the police will probably
never be known.

The Pahlers were well aware of what Elyse was like,
but they also knew that she deeply loved her family and
would never do anything to hurt them. They refused
point-blank to accept what others were implying.

The Pahlers even told police investigators about the
youths who pushed their daughter down the bank near
their home a few weeks before her disappearance. But
the boys were not interviewed.

At the bigger San Luis Obispo–based *Telegram Tribune*
newspaper staff photographer Robert Dyer was assigned
to copy photos of Elyse, and he got the clear impression

that police believed she was just another runaway.

"They took that attitude and, to be honest, it made me just presume she was as well," explained Dyer. "Even when I copied her picture, I wasn't too interested because I just thought she was yet another runaway."

There was never any question in the minds of the newspaper's editors, either. They had a policy of never doorstepping—cold calling—the families involved in such stories so the Pahlers were never even approached for a quote about what they thought might have happened to their daughter.

The sleepy, laid-back attitude of authorities in Arroyo Grande and San Luis Obispo County in general did nothing to help track down Elyse Pahler.

During those first few weeks after Elyse's disappearance, the family believed in their heart of hearts that something terrible had happened to their daughter. They listened to all the claims to the contrary but they would always ultimately come back to their original conclusion.

But, as the days turned into weeks, they started to wonder if maybe they were wrong and she had decided to abandon her family. After all, if Elyse had been killed, surely they would have found her body by now?

Eight

Joseph Fiorella, Jacob Delashmutt, and Royce Casey all had manic, drug-crazed expressions on their faces. They were staring down at Elyse Pahler's body as it lay propped against the fallen branch in the middle of that eucalyptus grove.

Just then one of them laughed. He laughed so hard that the other two boys joined in. It seemed as if they couldn't stop themselves.

Every time they looked down at the body, they felt overawed by what they had done. It had been one month since her death, but seeing her corpse lying there reminded them of the reality of their situation.

A friend of Fiorella and Delashmutt even recalled Fiorella telling him that he had committed "the ultimate sin to God" and that "they had bought their ticket to hell."

But the youths' visit back to the scene of their crime,

say prosecutors, was not merely to gloat at the terrible crime they had committed. They were trying to make sure that no one could see Elyse's body from the nearby road.

Later there was even talk of body parts being removed as part of some sick and twisted satanic ritual and rumors of sexual relations with the corpse. But all this still remains rumor.

Satisfied that the body would not be easily stumbled upon, the boys retreated back to Fiorella's house just a quarter of a mile across the windswept mesa.

In the weeks following Elyse's disappearance, her parents David and Lisanne spent much of their time trying to put together the pieces, to find the answers to the myriad of questions surrounding Elyse's vanishing. Their inability to understand their daughter's disappearance led to enormous guilt.

Were they to blame? And if so, what had they done wrong? What could they have done differently? Were they so preoccupied with their younger children that they had downplayed her problems with marijuana? Had they ignored Elyse to the point that their daughter felt unwanted?

The Pahlers questioned every aspect of their relationship with Elyse, but always returned to the same conclusion: Although there had certainly been problems, there was nothing that would force Elyse to run away.

Confused, David and Lisanne still refused to believe that their daughter's disappearance was related to anything going on at home. All they ever wanted to do was protect Elyse and give her the things she needed: a home, love, and a secure environment. If Elyse's disappearance was related to problems at home, the Pahlers thought, then they were failures as parents.

Desperate for results, the Pahler family launched their own independent hunt for Elyse. They hired a private detective to follow up what few leads there were and printed up thousands of flyers featuring a photo of their pretty missing teenage daughter. It had virtually the same information as the local newspaper article except that it clearly offered a reward to anyone who could help find Elyse.

When another teenage girl from Arroyo Grande disappeared amid apparently mysterious circumstances, many in the town became convinced that the two cases were connected. But that rapidly proved not to be the case because the other girl was eventually located.

Frustrated by the apparent lack of police interest, the Pahlers urged their private investigator to start following up any leads—however vague—concerning their missing daughter in the hope that one might lead to the other.

The strongest clue remained the disappearance of that twenty-year-old male neighbor at about the same time as Elyse. The Pahlers had grown increasingly convinced that the youth was connected to Elyse in some way. It was a straw of hope to clasp onto, and they were not going to just let it slip through their hands.

Eventually the missing youth was traced to Indonesia, and the private detective even flew to southeast Asia to interview him. But it soon became clear he had nothing to do with the case, and everyone concluded that his involvement had all been a very unfortunate red herring.

"The police tried a bit harder after this, but they still didn't even bother to search the area near Elyse's home with dogs or anything," recalled Elyse's friend Angel Katyryni.

It was a difficult situation for the police. In that area of California alone more than a dozen teenagers went missing every week, and most eventually turned up a few weeks, months, or even years later. They had judged Elyse's case accordingly, and concluded that there was little or nothing they could do to find her. They fully appreciated the attitude of her parents, but there was no concrete evidence that Elyse Pahler had come to any harm.

In late August, 1995—more than six weeks after Elyse's disappearance—her two close friends Angel and Shannon went camping with some friends at nearby Lopez Lake, east of Arroyo Grande.

The girls had originally planned the night out long before Elyse went missing, and they were well aware that she should have been there with them. "It made it kinda sad in a way 'cause Elyse wasn't with us," recalled Angel.

The weather that night was swelteringly hot, and there was a never-ending invasion of hungry flies skimming off the surface of the lake toward any food left lying nearby. Armies of red ants and mosquitoes paraded across the ground at regular intervals.

Shannon, Angel, and two other girlfriends were sitting around a table outside their tent watching the sun slowly dipping behind the nearby mountains, when they heard the sound of a truck straining to get up the hilly track that led to the campsite.

Eventually a red, rusting truck came over the horizon, moving rapidly in their direction. The girls strained to see who was in the vehicle. It was being driven by Travis Williams. Crammed next to him were Royce Casey, Jacob Delashmutt, and Joe Fiorella.

They appeared to switch direction and head for another part of the campsite, but then one of the boys pointed at the girls. The truck fishtailed before heading toward them. The sound of death metal music surged out of the vehicle as it screeched to a halt. With the music still blaring, Delashmutt rolled down the window and shouted:

"Hey. You girls at Arroyo High?"

Shannon and Angel nodded reluctantly. It seemed a cheap pick-up line, especially since they already knew the boys slightly. These were, after all, the same youths who'd starred on their not-to-meet-in-a-dark-alleyway list.

As the girls hesitated about replying to the boys, the thudding death metal beats coming from inside the cab of the truck added to an uncomfortable atmosphere.

Just then Williams, the driver, yanked his hand brake on and switched off the rumbling engine. All four boys jumped out. Their eyes seemed glazed, and they were all staring in the direction of Shannon and Angel.

There was an eerie beat of silence the moment the music died.

"There was no one else to talk to, so we decided to let them come over," Angel later explained.

The youths stumbled awkwardly toward the table where Shannon and Angel were sitting. ''Their eyes were beady, and they had clearly been drinking,'' added Angel.

She noticed that Joe Fiorella's eyes never left her as they walked over.

Just then Delashmutt spoke.

''Hey. Aren't you friends with that girl Elyse?''

Both girls said yes.

''What d'you think happened to her?''

Angel spoke up.

''Something bad. I just know it. She was my best friend.''

Delashmutt: ''What d'you mean—bad?''

''Maybe she went off with that guy who lived up the street and maybe he killed her.''

''Wow. Heavy duty.''

Delashmutt hesitated for a beat and turned toward the others.

''Do you *really* think that happened to her?''

He seemed to be smirking.

A wall of silence came over the group, only broken when Delashmutt spoke up again.

''You wanna go for a walk?''

Shannon turned to Angel and shrugged her shoulders. Angel wanted to say something because she knew these very same boys had forced Elyse down that bank near her house a few weeks before she disappeared.

But Angel was afraid to say anything in front of them. She felt scared although she wasn't completely sure why.

Delashmutt repeated his request.

"Come on, girls, it's a beautiful evening for a walk."

Shannon turned to Angel and shrugged her shoulders. "Why not?"

Angel whispered, "No way." She should have stopped her friend, but she was too afraid to say anything. She didn't really know why she felt that way.

Shannon got up from the bench table and walked off with the four boys along a winding path that led through the woods on the edge of the campsite.

Within minutes Shannon was aware that Joe Fiorella's eyes were constantly boring into her as the group moved along that pathway, but Jacob Delashmutt and Royce Casey were talking so much that she didn't have the time to consider why he was so hyped up.

"You really think something happened to Elyse?" asked Casey awkwardly.

"I know Elyse, and she wouldn't have just gone without letting us know."

"That's real scary," said Delashmutt. He sounded to Shannon as if he really cared, but she didn't much like the way Williams and Fiorella were acting. She looked across at all of the boys one by one, and concluded it was time to get back to her friends, whom she could still see in the distance.

Shannon turned around and started to pull away from the youths. Joe Fiorella's eyes were even more beady by this stage, and they continued following her every movement.

"Hey. Where you goin'?" chipped in Delashmutt.

"Gotta get back to my friends," replied Shannon.

"You wanna come to a party tonight?" asked Delashmutt.

"No thanks."

Shannon felt a strange sense of relief when she got back to Angel and her two other girlfriends at their tent. It was as if the boys had been trying to find out something, but she wasn't entirely sure what they'd wanted.

More than a year later, Shannon reflected on that strange encounter.

"When I think back on it, it was real scary. They'd all been doing drugs, and their breath smelt real bad of alcohol. But it was Joey who scared me the most—he seemed completely crazed."

Elyse Pahler's best friend Angel Katyryni woke up with a sudden jolt upward, snapped open her eyes, and just sat there for a few minutes thinking about what she feared might have happened to Elyse.

She had been sleeping badly ever since that encounter with the youths at the campsite. She kept wondering if they had some involvement in her disappearance, but she had absolutely no concrete evidence to suggest they were.

Angel was puzzled as to why those boys, none of whom she knew really well, kept starring so vividly in her dreams. Often she'd lie in her bed and try to get back to sleep, but it was impossible because her mind was racing.

She kept thinking back to those boys. Why were they so significant? What was it about them that had been so scary?

Angel thought about how the boys had knocked Elyse down that bank near her home. Angel started to wonder whether perhaps they were involved with her disappearance.

She hadn't even thought about the significance of the incident in the few days after Elyse's disappearance. But now it suddenly seemed important.

Later that same day, Angel contacted the Arroyo Grande Police Department and told them all about that incident involving Delashmutt, Fiorella, and Casey. The deputy who interviewed Angel over the telephone listened patiently to what she had to say, but he didn't seem very interested. He apparently never conveyed the story to anyone else, so he remained completely unaware that Elyse's parents had told a similar account a few weeks earlier.

The police remained convinced that Elyse had run away from home, and the case was left on a pending file. There wasn't the personnel at the police department to start spending valuable man hours on what was clearly a missing persons' case.

That call to the police was about the closest Angel got to saying she thought Delashmutt, Casey, and Fiorella were involved. When the police didn't seem to respond, she realized that she and Shannon were all alone in their suspicions. She had no idea that the Pahlers were also aware of the youths' existence.

Those boys had acted really suspiciously on one hand, and the police were not believing them on the other. What else could they do?

Meanwhile others from Arroyo Grande High School were facing a dilemma.

"A number of them thought they knew that those guys were involved, but they were afraid to tell anyone. They could not inform their parents, and the police probably wouldn't believe them anyway," explained one friend.

Shannon Plotner and Angel Katyryni had already decided not to mention their suspicions to anyone else again.

Nine

Less than a month after that incident at the campsite, Shannon and Angel were in the school yard talking to some friends, when they became aware that Joe Fiorella was standing right next to them. He was clearly trying to listen to their conversation.

"We just moved away, but it was kinda strange. He seemed very nervous," recalled Shannon.

At first Fiorella tried to stay close to the girls, but then he got the message and moved away.

Not long after this, Fiorella and Delashmutt tried to muscle in on Shannon and Angel's conversation in the school yard. As was so often the case at the time, Elyse was the main subject being discussed.

"Everyone in the school had a different theory as to where she might have gone," explained Angel. "And we were all talking about her when Jacob and Joe tried to step into our group."

Initially the two boys said little as Shannon, Angel, and their friends talked about what they believed had happened to Elyse.

Then one girl said she reckoned Elyse had been murdered.

The two boys visibly winced. ''They looked real uncomfortable,'' said Shannon.

Then Delashmutt butted in.

''She's gone off with a guy. She couldn't get enough of it. She was a horny bitch.''

Shannon and Angel were stunned by this comment because they had thought Delashmutt hardly knew Elyse.

''They tried to make out Elyse would sleep with any boy, and she'd got what she deserved,'' recalled Angel.

''We were really pissed at him for saying that, especially since he wasn't even a close friend. A lot of us believed Elyse was dead, but we didn't know why or how.

''Some kids said that maybe she'd gone to a late night party, and someone killed her and hid her body someplace.

''But whatever we thought, he had no right making those comments. It was totally out of line.''

A few days later Delashmutt wandered alongside Shannon as she was leaving school one afternoon and tried to hit on her.

''Hey, you wanna come out with me?''

Shannon ignored him at first.

''Come on. I know you want to.''

Shannon smiled hesitantly, but still ignored Delashmutt.

"You know my friend Royce Casey at Lopez, don't you?"

Shannon tried to walk faster in order to get away from him.

"So what?"

"I want to share you with my friend Casey. Come on," pressed Delashmutt.

This time Shannon could not stop herself.

"Take a hike, you creep."

Jacob Delashmutt gave up on trying to ask Shannon out after her strong rebuttal, but that didn't stop him approaching other girls at Arroyo Grande High School for a date.

Shannon explained, "Jacob was hitting on girls all the time. He seemed desperate."

Shannon also noticed that nearly all the girls were blond, blue-eyed, and pretty. Not until many months later did it dawn on her that many of them actually looked a lot like her missing friend, Elyse Pahler.

Not long afterward Jacob Delashmutt was expelled from Arroyo Grande High School for persistently being absent. His behavior had steadily worsened since returning to school after that long summer break. Some of his classmates said he seemed totally distracted and very short-tempered.

"He was a troubled soul. He was never cool about anything. It was obvious he had a lot on his mind," said one student who knew Delashmutt.

Another classmate said that Delashmutt had become increasingly sensitive to criticism from anyone. "He was

real paranoid about everything. We kinda steered clear
of him most of the time.''

In September, 1995, under pressure from the Pahler family, the Arroyo Grande police stepped up pleas for information about Elyse's disappearance.

Hundreds more of the yellow flyers featuring a photo
of the pretty teenager were distributed throughout the
south county.

And police even received a number of reported sightings of Elyse, which led detectives to believe she was
still alive and well, living in San Luis Obispo County.

One former neighbor of the Pahlers even reported seeing someone who looked like Elyse sitting in a car near
her former home in Arroyo Grande.

All these reports had a detrimental effect on the Pahlers' relationship with many of Elyse's friends. They
started to wonder if many of them actually knew where
their beloved daughter was and were protecting her
through some misguided loyalty.

On September 30, 1995, Joe Fiorella's best friend Travis
Williams allegedly shot dead seventy-five-year-old Mabel Agueda at her home in Arroyo Grande.

According to prosecutors, eighteen-year-old Williams
and another youth killed the old lady while they were
robbing her house.

The arrest of Williams shortly after the homicide had
the knock-on effect of scaring Fiorella, Delashmutt, and
Casey because they all knew that Williams was one of

the few people who knew exactly what had happened to Elyse Pahler.

At Arroyo Grande High School, Williams' arrest on suspicion of homicide was the talk of just about every classroom. But then certain schoolchildren began saying that his arrest was just the tip of the iceberg.

"People were saying that his friends Delashmutt and Fiorella had got into some really weird shit," explained one classmate at the school. "The rumor was that they'd killed a girl after sacrificing her to the devil."

Even though word of the alleged ritual spread, the students kept the stories away from the ears and eyes of any adults. The killers were among them there at that school, but no one had the courage to do anything about it.

"I think many believed there was some kind of test of loyalty about the whole business. No one wanted to be the one who told on the boys. Also many of us were real afraid of what they might do to us," added the classmate.

By Christmastime, Elyse's family became convinced they were the only ones who still cared about what had happened to the fifteen-year-old schoolgirl.

Even curious local newspaper journalists were given the clear impression she was nothing more than yet another runaway.

"The police were saying she was a runaway. We all presumed they were correct," explained San Luis Obispo news photographer Robert Dyer.

He was even assigned the task of photographing a new flyer for his newspaper

"When I took a photo of Elyse's flyer, I thought, 'I'll take the picture but she's just a runaway. She'll turn up sooner or later.' "

It was an especially difficult time for Elyse's parents as their minds raced through various theories as to what might have happened to her. Perhaps their daughter's friends were protecting Elyse and knew exactly where she was?

Some of her friends became convinced the family thought they were hiding something from them.

Recalled Shannon, "I'm certain they reckoned we'd been in touch with Elyse, but of course we hadn't. It made it kinda difficult talking to them."

David Pahler was so convinced by one tip-off that he even staked out a house in Arroyo Grande where Elyse was supposed to be staying.

Elyse's disappearance added to the conviction that the Pahlers were right to move out of rural Arroyo Grande. In the previous eighteen months there had been numerous incidents such as gangs in cars frightening children by following them home.

Lisanne Pahler remained convinced that the incident when the boys pushed Elyse down the bank was significant, but she believed the youths' involvement must have been discounted by police, whom she presumed had interviewed the boys after the Pahlers told them about the incident near their home.

The Pahlers believed that before her disappearance, Elyse had succumbed to what her parents considered was undesirable peer pressure from school acquaintances.

Elyse's experimentations with soft drugs and numerous dates with local boys was sufficient evidence in their eyes of the bad influences surrounding their daughter.

Ironically, it had been those fears that contributed toward their move to the country club area of San Luis Obispo just one month after Elyse's disappearance.

However, the move itself brought with it a sense of isolation, which made the family even more convinced that nothing was being done to find their daughter.

Around this time the family received a series of phone calls suggesting Elyse was alive. One caller claimed she had been spotted in San Luis Obispo with a man. Another said she was alive and well in nearby Avil Beach. Others claimed that she'd been seen in other states and even another country.

"Each lead brought us hope we'd have her back again," her mother Lisanne later recalled. Although in her heart of hearts she found it difficult to imagine anything but the worst.

At her ranch in Santa Ynez, Elyse's grandmother, Elyse Neilsen Walter, contacted missing persons organizations throughout the country and traveled hundreds of miles following up possible clues about Elyse's movements.

But she was rapidly concluding that "someone knew something about what happened that night, but no one was talking." She had the distinct impression that many of Elyse's school aquaintances knew where the fifteen-year-old was.

That was the key frustration for the family. They suspected that a number of local children knew precisely where Elyse had gone, but no one was saying anything— whether that was through some misguided sense of loyalty or just plain stupidity was difficult to gauge.

"It was infuriating," added Mrs. Walter, "to know

that others must have known all along what had happened.''

In January, 1996, Elyse's grandmother felt so overwhelmed with concern that she decided to write an open letter to her granddaughter in the local newspaper. It said:

> "*I miss you—and I love you! Everyone is very worried and heartbroken because we don't know how you are—if you are happy, warm, well fed, and healthy.*
>
> "*I promise you, I do not want to 'drag' you home—or anything even like that.*
>
> "*I just want us to sit down and talk and hug! Please! Please! Just call me so we can know you are alive.*
>
> "*My love always, Nana.*"

Meanwhile, Delashmutt and Fiorella continued to regularly watch their favorite movie, *River's Edge*, starring Keanu Reeves.

But the difference was that each time they saw it, following Elyse Pahler's disappearance, it seemed even more real. They actually related to everything that was happening on-screen.

When the character who'd murdered his girl classmate talked in one scene about the power he felt having killed, the boys felt even more awesome about what they had done.

> "*I had total control of her. It felt so real. She was dead—right there in front of me, and I felt so fuck-*

ing alive. Funny thing is, I'm dead now. They're going to fry me . . ."

Whether they felt a twinge of guilt like the character in the movie will probably never be known.

But one of their friends explained, "They were completely wrapped up in that movie. It became like a blueprint for their life. They never stopped talking about it in class. We all thought it was a bit weird to say the least."

Ten

Royce Casey, nervous, seventeen, and on the verge of being a high school dropout, had had minor brushes with the law since junior high, mainly due to his propensity for drugs and alcohol.

With his long dark hair and nervy smile, Casey was eager for people to like him. His moral lapses resulted from weakness, not malice. He had a habit of following others even though he was often the oldest in the pack.

But now Casey could not shake the nervous, painful ache in his stomach. Ever since that murderous night in July, 1995, he had found it hard to eat or sleep. He didn't want to believe he was involved. But it was gradually dawning on him that there was no escape.

By January, 1996, Casey had actually managed to ingratiate himself to Elyse Pahler's best friend Angel Katyryni. It may have been his way of feeling better about what had happened to Elyse Pahler rather than anything more sinister.

Angel soon concluded that Casey seemed the nicest of the bunch despite that scary meeting when he and the other boys had turned up at the campsite the previous August.

"He was more gentle and didn't seem as freaky as the others," recalled Angel.

Even though she had reservations about the boys and kept wondering if they had been involved in Elyse's disappearance, Angel decided to give Casey the benefit of the doubt.

She sometimes even shared a coffee and a milk shake with him at the Burger King in Arroyo Grande.

"We talked about lots of things, including Elyse. He seemed genuinely upset about what had happened to her. I thought that was kinda sweet considering he hardly knew her."

Casey also told Angel that his friend Jacob Delashmutt had grown increasingly weird in the previous few months, and he was trying to avoid him and the other boys in their group.

Casey said that all of them—Casey, Delashmutt, Fiorella, and Travis Williams—had got into satanism, and they had even broken into a graveyard and circled the stones of graves that they eventually intended to rob of bodies.

"I thought that was so weird," explained Angel. "And Royce seemed to be, like, trying to get away from them."

Casey even told Angel he was too scared to completely cut off his friends because "they might do something to me if I dump them."

At home Casey's family noticed that the teenager was far from happy. He would spend days on end locked in his bedroom writing pages and pages in a special journal he had kept since the disappearance of Elyse Pahler.

The misspelled, profanity-laced diary would eventually shed some insight into the terrible crime Casey and his two friends allegedly committed. He described how he was "fighting on the other side now [where] satans arised and shall conquer and reign. . . . " Incredibly, he suggested that "psycho cerial killers" should "build an alter of sacrifice," noting that "virgin meat is the ultimate sacrifice."

At the Lopez High School, Casey continued writing his journal. Pouring out his weird, Satan-obsessed innermost feelings into the book seemed to ease the fear he constantly felt about what the future had in store for him.

Gradually, the journal he had begun in October, 1995, became more wracked with guilt. Casey then joined the New Life Ministry Church in nearby Pismo Beach. He seemed so troubled that one of the ministers took a personal interest in his well-being.

One day in early March, 1996, Royce Casey told one of the ministers he'd done something very bad and wondered if God would ever forgive him. But when pressed, he refused to elaborate.

Some days after Casey's aborted "confession," someone called the Arroyo Grande Police Department.

"I have some information about the missing schoolgirl, Elyse Pahler," said the caller. "She's dead."

Just then the line went dead. The only detective available when the call was put through was well aware of the missing teenager, but hadn't been directly involved in the case. He soon established there had been more than a dozen similar calls since Elyse had disappeared the previous July.

It seemed that some in Arroyo Grande did indeed feel guilty that they knew about the disappearance of Elyse Pahler, and wanted to get it off their chests.

The detective hung up the telephone. He didn't believe Elyse Pahler had been murdered. It was probably a case of some kids playing a prank or someone trying to give the police a bum steer because the missing girl wanted her parents to stop trying to find her.

No action was taken, and the case of missing teenager Elyse's name and personal details remained on the police files to await further action.

Meanwhile the other boys in the group were reacting in different ways to the stress and strain of hiding the secret of what had really happened to Elyse Pahler.

Jacob Delashmutt continued to be the confident, talkative one. He was always asking girls out on dates, even though he and his friends were definitely not considered good catches.

In the early part of 1996—many months after Elyse's disappearance—one of Angel's girlfriends at school slept with Delashmutt in exchange for some crank. "It was a sick thing to do," recalled Angel. "She said Jacob was real weird in bed and when he took drugs he got even more weird."

Delashmutt's artistic skills were also causing quite a

lot of attention at school. He was drawing swastika and "SS" type signs all over his own schoolbooks. It got so bad that some of his teachers insisted he stop the habit because Jewish members of the staff were finding it offensive.

Joseph Fiorella remained coldly detached about everything, retreating to his dark bedroom and no doubt reading about Satan. He still remembered vividly what had happened that night with Elyse Pahler, but he didn't show any guilt about it.

In some ways Fiorella appeared to feel stronger as a result of what had happened. It made him feel important, and he liked the fact that he knew what had happened to Elyse.

Sometimes he was tempted to return to the eucalyptus grove and take a look at the evidence of his spiritual supremacy. No one knows to this day how often the group returned.

Delashmutt and Fiorella were consuming ever increasing quantities of drugs and retreating to the Pipe of Death whenever they wanted to escape authority and the tedium of life in Arroyo Grande.

On February 21, 1996, two Arroyo Grande High School students, Matthew Schandel, eighteen, and Joshua Garner, seventeen, attempted to rob and murder a forty-nine-year-old woman at her Arroyo Grande home.

Schandel and Garner both knew Candace Calder, and had even made a phone call from a public telephone in a nearby shopping center to make sure she was alone before they carried out the attack.

Dressed in ski masks and armed with an aluminum

baseball bat, they climbed over the fence behind Calder's house and entered the home through an open garage door.

When Calder discovered the two teenagers in her home, Schandel started swinging the bat at her. When she tried to escape, Garner grabbed her as Schandel continued hitting her. Calder suffered a broken arm and thumb and fractured skull. The assault was so furious that at one stage Schandel hit his accomplice Garner by accident.

The incident effectively grabbed a lot of the attention from the fast fading story of the disappearance of Elyse Pahler and the homicide allegedly committed by Travis Williams. It became the main talking point at Arroyo Grande High School.

A week after the robbery and attempted murder incident, Elyse Neilson Walter put up new flyers, offering a $1,000 reward in a desperate attempt to make sure the public did not completely forget about her granddaughter.

When Royce Casey spotted one of the posters with Elyse's photograph in the center of Arroyo Grande, it sent a shiver up his spine.

Meanwhile Joe Fiorella was once again misbehaving at Arroyo Grande High School. The teachers told his mom, Betsy Leo, they could no longer handle the wayward teenager. At the end of February, 1996, he was expelled from the school for the second time.

His mother assured authorities she would school her son at home from then on. No one seemed to mind. There was just a sense of relief that he had left the school without causing any serious incidents.

Eleven

It was the shape of her eyes that Royce Casey couldn't forget. That image of her lying there among the broken branches dominated his mind. It had haunted him day and night, but when he saw her photo on that poster it sent him over the edge.

His writings in his journal were supposed to ease the pain. But instead, every time he poured out his feelings, the guilt just got worse and worse.

Casey began attending the New Life Ministry, in nearby Pismo Beach, even more regularly. He had rejoined the church's youth ministry because he felt so troubled by what had happened that night in July the previous year when Elyse Pahler had been killed.

Then one day he went one step further than he had before by bringing up the subject of good and evil.

"Do you think a person is basically damned forever?'' he asked one of the ministers during a question-and-answer session at the church one day.

Casey continued, ''Can God forgive anything?''

''Of course he can forgive anything,'' came the minister's reply.

Casey left the meeting that day slightly happier because he started to wonder if perhaps he was wrong to feel such remorse and regret for what he had been involved with. He let the minister's advice sit for a while.

But the vision of what happened that night on the Nipomo Mesa would not go away.

Some time later he returned to the New Life Ministry and started to ask some even more pointed questions that were undoubtedly connected to Elyse's death.

Eventually he realized he had no choice, and told the minister he had to unburden himself of something very horrible that had happened.

The advice he got was that confession was good for the soul.

Casey poured out all his feelings and some crucial details of what happened the night Elyse Pahler was killed.

He begged God's forgiveness but knew in his heart of hearts that he would have to tell the authorities what had happened. In many ways he thought life might improve after that.

There was certainly no way he could continue his tortured path holding down such a deep and dark secret. It had effectively ruined his life; he couldn't concentrate on anything other than the dreadful killing of Elyse. His schoolwork was abysmal. He had virtually stopped seeing his friends. He was also mightily fearful that some of the others might kill him if they heard he had started talking to people about what really happened that night.

The only escape was to tell the police the truth.

So on March 13, 1996, Royce Casey walked into Arroyo Grande Police Station and made a full confession to his part in the killing of Elyse Pahler. He believed he had no choice.

A few hours later the teenager led investigators to the spot in that dense eucalyptus grove where he believed the remains of Elyse Pahler would be found—just a quarter of a mile from her home at the time.

All those rumors about sightings in Pismo Beach and other seaside resorts had given false hope to her family and friends. Now the truth was about to be revealed for the first time.

In the crowded training room on the second floor of the Arroyo Grande Police Station, excitement and anticipation were high. Detectives and patrolmen mixed in small groups, discussing their ideas on what should be done. It was an incongruous gathering for the station.

The mood was serious but upbeat. There was planning ahead, as well as politics to overcome. Several questions remained unanswered. What department was going to handle the investigation? Who was going to interview whom?

The body of Elyse Pahler had been found in San Luis Obispo County and, most agreed, the murder probably had occurred there, too. That meant the San Luis Obispo County Sheriff Department had jurisdiction.

Armed with a full confession from Royce Casey, sher-

iff's detectives arrested him. Joe Fiorella and Jacob Delashmutt would follow.

"It's a complex case," Sheriff Ed Williams told his
men. He had already assigned six detectives to interview
witnesses.

Williams also confirmed that his deputies had found
the body of Elyse Pahler near the 2400 block of Chamisal Lane on the Nipomo Mesa.

The only thing Williams requested was a little time.
Two of his detectives were still at the autopsy.

No one knew what to expect. Several considerations
remained. How would the two other suspects react?
Would the boys resist? The detectives discussed the lay-
outs of their residences and how they would proceed.
Precautions needed to be taken; both situations could be
volatile.

About ten minutes later, they headed out to the boys'
homes.

An unmarked car pulled up in front of the Fiorella's
apartment complex just a quarter of a mile from the spot
where Elyse Pahler's body had been discovered. Two
patrolmen in marked units followed closely behind.

Within minutes they had detained Joe Fiorella and ad-
vised his mom Betsy Leo to accompany them back to
the station. During the short ride back to the station,
Fiorella was full of questions. Fiorella knew what he was
doing. He was trying to find out how much the police
actually knew.

Fiorella and his mom were escorted past several detectives and patrolmen who were still gathered in the
training room. Everyone wanted to be involved in the

case. Fiorella was placed in a small interview room with a glass window that faced across the hall to other small cubicles.

A detective and two uniformed police arrived at the Arroyo Grande home of Jacob Delashmutt at about the same time Joe Fiorella was being picked up.

"One of you go around back in case he tries to run," the detective told one of the other officers.

The detective and the other officer walked to the entrance to the apartment and knocked on the door. When Delashmutt emerged, he wanted to know what was going on. The detective would only say that he needed to come down to the police station.

Delashmutt rode silently in the backseat, his hands folded in his lap, as the three police officers rode back to the police station. The youth was then walked upstairs to a small windowless interview room on the juvenile side of the building. Delashmutt did not know that Joe Fiorella was down the hall being questioned by detectives.

In contrast to Fiorella and Delashmutt, Royce Casey seemed almost relieved at the chance to talk about Elyse's death. The burden seemed too great for him to bear. Within a short time he had admitted everything to county DA investigator Doug Odom. Casey was remorseful, composed, and cooperative. He wasn't the typical tough teenager on a macho power trip. There was something sad about this boy.

Casey's head dropped as he was read his constitutional rights.

"Do you understand your rights?" Odom asked him.

"Yes."

"And you know you have the right to have either or both your parents here? Or anyone else of your choosing?"

"Yes, but I don't want either of my parents here," Casey said. "I'll keep on talking to you, but I don't want them here."

Doug Odom then moved toward the tape recorder at the edge of the desk.

"We need to get this down on tape, Royce," said the investigator.

Casey nodded his head as Odom slid his chair around the table so there was nothing between the two of them. He looked at the teenager, whose head remained lowered.

"Royce," said Odom. "Royce, look at me. I think it would make you feel a lot better if you would just tell us what happened. Who used the knife on Elyse?"

Over the following few hours, Royce Casey described how they took Elyse to the eucalyptus grove, fed her with drugs, tied the belt around her neck, and then stabbed her.

Eventually Doug Odom had a signed statement from Casey, implicating Fiorella and Delashmutt.

At that, Odom, in the interview room, looked at his colleagues in repugnant disbelief. At least a minute of silence followed.

Then the investigators checked to see whether Casey had a belt or shoestrings—anything he might use to kill himself. He didn't. Then they walked to the door, looked back at Casey for a moment, then left the room.

Fiorella and Delashmutt were teenagers, street punks at worst. Mixed-up kids in a sleepy community at best. Casey, on the other hand, was intelligent, sensitive, and very weak. He was the key to the police investigation.

When the investigators returned to the interview room, Casey was still sitting in the same position. They knew they had to be gentle with him because he was the one who'd provide them with all the vital evidence.

By the time they left once more, Casey began to cry, slowly and without sound. His face was crumpled in anguish. He slumped forward, holding his face in his hands, and cried slowly, giving in to the nervous tension. He wrung his hands. He was scared, terrified. Not for himself, but he feared the other two would never forgive him.

Other investigators returned to each of the suspects a few minutes later and took them downstairs to the booking room separately, where a uniformed officer prepared to photograph and fingerprint them.

"What's going to happen now?" one of them asked a police officer.

"You will be transported to the Juvenile Services Center. There will probably be a hearing on Monday."

To the side of the booking room, the relatives of the three boys were gathered. Some were crying.

Minutes later a convoy of marked police vehicles transported the relatives back to their homes as the boys prepared for their first night of incarceration.

Investigators knew their inquiries had only just begun.

Twelve

On Friday, March 15, Elyse's close friends Angel Katyryni and Shannon Plotner arrived as usual for first period at Arroyo Grande High School.

As they were waiting for their teacher to start the class, one of the boys in the class turned to Shannon.

"Hey. You know they cut your friend's head off."

Shannon hesitated for a moment.

"What are you talking about?"

"Your friend Elyse. They found her body over by Chamisal Lane yesterday."

Shannon tried to absorb the meaning of those words, but she couldn't.

"You're kidding me?"

The boy smirked at her.

It was then she knew it must be true.

Shannon rushed over to Angel, and they both burst into tears.

Just then another boy walked over to the two hysterical girls.

"They cut the head clean off. Weird."

For the following few minutes, numerous pupils made sick and completely inaccurate claims about the injuries sustained by Elyse during the murderous attack.

The two girls were excused from class for the day and went home to cry. They didn't go back to school for two weeks.

"It was bad enough hearing that Elyse was dead, without all the sick comments. In some ways that got to us more than Elyse's murder. It was real upsetting," Shannon later recalled.

But even worse, some at Arroyo Grande High were trying to elevate Jacob Delashmutt to hero status.

"Some of the kids were saying they knew Jacob just to be macho. They were trying to make him into this kinda sick hero. It was weird," added Shannon.

Most disturbing of all, many students at the high school were not surprised that Delashmutt, Casey, and Fiorella had been arrested—because many of them actually knew what had happened to Elyse, but were too afraid to tell the authorities.

"Some of them even said that the boys had been asking around who were the virgins because they wanted one to sacrifice," added Shannon.

"I just don't understand why they didn't say anything earlier."

San Luis Obispo *Telegram-Tribune* staff photographer Robert Dyer had been enjoying a cup of coffee a couple of hours after coming on shift at 10:00 A.M. when his city editor told him to head down to the Nipoma Mesa area of Arroyo Grande because a body had been uncovered by police.

"Apparently someone's already placed flowers at the site. Could be great material for the front page," he told his photographer.

Dyer—a tall, thin, scholarly looking fellow with spectacles—was given an approximate location of where the body had been found, and was told to get down there as soon as possible.

Coming off Highway 101 and then onto Interstate 1, Dyer immediately noted the sea of eucalyptus groves on both sides of the road. They were planted in perfect rows with dirt tracks leading through them toward the occasional house.

"I remember thinking there must be many more bodies hidden up there. It was the perfect place to dump a corpse. Nobody ever goes along those tracks, because most people don't want to risk getting stuck," recalled Dyer.

For more than thirty minutes Dyer screeched up and down various dirt roads trying to find a clue as to where Elyse's body had been found. Then he saw a TV van coming out of a track alongside the main road. He immediately headed across to where the vehicle had emerged from, and stumbled upon the tracks left a few hours earlier by the sheriff's vehicles. Despite the fact Elyse's body had only just been removed, not even the yellow crime scene plastic tape remained.

Dyer got out of his car on the edge of the eucalyptus grove and started off through the dense undergrowth. There was an eerie silence enveloping the area, with no sounds other than the mesa wind whistling around his

ankles. The only building in the distance was a solitary
white-board house. "It was very spooky and scary. I felt
very uncomfortable" was how he later recalled that day.

A few minutes after entering the grove, Dyer found
himself climbing quite a steep hill before coming across
an area where the ground had clearly been disturbed.
Dyer walked gingerly around it and looked for foot-
prints. He immediately recognized the sheriff's boot
marks, and realized from the position of those prints
exactly where Elyse Pahler's body had lain for eight
months unnoticed.

Dyer stayed at the scene for twenty minutes while he
took a series of photographs from all possible angles.
The sunlight was barely peeping through the eucalyptus
trees, which had grown so densely that they virtually
enclosed the entire grove.

Dyer also noticed evidence of the TV crews, who he'd
seen driving in the opposite direction as he entered the
area a few minutes earlier.

Some flowers had been put on a large branch that lay
across the shrubbery. It was the branch Elyse's body had
been propped against and abused by her attackers, following her brutal stabbing.

After seventeen years as a press photographer, Dyer
was well used to attending major scenes of death and
destruction, but there was something about this death
scene that seemed more tragic than all the others put
together.

"I just wanted to get the hell out of there as quickly
as possible. I felt like an intruder at a shrine."

Elyse's uncle, Joe Pahler, of Paso Robles, found himself
acting as unofficial spokesman for the Pahlers when re-

porters began swamping the family with calls. He informed newsmen that dental records had not yet been compared to confirm his niece's identity.

Elyse's parents, David and Lisanne, remained far too grief-stricken to talk about the killing.

"This is such a sad situation," explained Joe Pahler to inquiring journalists.

By Friday, March 15—the day after the discovery of Elyse's body—official identification had still not been carried out, and Dave and Lisanne Pahler continued to hold out hope that it might not be her after all.

It was not until the morning of Monday, March 18, 1996, that the Elyse Pahler murder story exploded in the San Luis Obispo County area press, banner headlined by even the most conservative newspapers.

Over the next few weeks, it was to become a journalistic bonanza that became richer by the hour as swarms of reporters began digging into the backgrounds of the victim and her alleged killers.

The reality was succinctly stated in the headline from that day's *Five Cities Times Press Recorder*:

MISSING GIRL FOUND DEAD; BOYS ARRESTED

David Pahler was particularly upset by this news story because it incorrectly identified him as Elyse's stepfather.

A forensic scientist was due to perform a full autopsy on the body the following Monday to confirm how she died and whether it was Elyse.

Until then the sheriff's Sergeant Rob Reid said he would not release any more information about the case. The identification of the boys arrested in connection with Elyse's death was still not being officially confirmed at this stage.

Back at the Pahler home, Elyse's sisters Jenilee, fourteen, and Kristina, seven, plus brother Ryan, twelve, were distraught about the news.

But the Pahler parents, Dave and Lisanne, felt an underlying anger with authorities, who for months had tried to convince them that Elyse had run away.

"Elyse's death brought it all home to them. They kept wondering why the police didn't search the area for Elyse. It made everything seem even worse," explained one family member.

But the Pahlers held back their anger and tried desperately to remember the good times with Elyse.

Lisanne Pahler said: "She loved us. She always had a big smile. She wasn't an 'in-your-face' type of kid.

"She had this great uplifting personality. She had big hopes and dreams. She wanted to be an actress, a singer in a band, an artist, and someday a mother."

David Pahler recalled how Elyse had once said that she wanted everyone in the country to eventually know her name. "She wanted to be famous."

It was a tragic epitaph.

On Monday, March 18, the news none of the Pahlers wanted confirmed came through; the young girl's body found in that eucalyptus grove on the Nipomo Mesa was Elyse. Her identification was established through her dental records.

Cause of death had not yet been determined, as forensic experts were continuing their autopsy.

The following day's *Telegram-Tribune* named the three boys—Royce E. Casey, seventeen, Jacob W. Delashmutt, sixteen, and Joseph L. Fiorella, fifteen—for the first time. They all faced charges of murder. The district attorney had filed a petition asking the court to certify that all three should be tried as adults.

Sheriff Ed Williams told the newspaper that all the defendants knew the victim, and confirmed that one of them had led detectives to Elyse's body.

Williams told newsmen he would not release any more information until his department's investigation was completed. He also asked others in his department, as well as Elyse's parents, not to discuss any details of the case.

David Pahler's only comment to the press at that time was that the boys were not close friends of his daughter's. "She rode the school bus with them, and that's how they knew each other. There might have been some kind of superficial friendship, but that's the extent of it as far as we know."

Since the discovery of Elyse's body the previous Thursday, the family had received hundreds of condolence calls from friends and strangers, including Elyse's girlfriends, along with Arroyo Grande High School students and teachers as well as representatives of several church groups.

"Many of her friends have told us how Elyse changed their lives," explained her father. "They tell stories of how she encouraged them to draw and to write poetry, how she spurred them on. One girl said Elyse had 'electrified' her and made her life better.''

David Pahler genuinely felt that it was the warmth of others that was helping the family get through their terrible ordeal.

''We're a Christian family. We believe Elyse is in heaven with her cousins and paternal grandmother, and everything is fine there. This is what is carrying us through this hard time.''

The following day, the first disturbing details of how Elyse was killed were revealed by forensic experts.

It emerged that she had died of multiple stab wounds to her torso and may have been tortured as well.

Deputy District Attorney Dan Bouchard said the charges against the boys had been enhanced with ''special circumstances''—allegations of torture and excessive cruelty as well as the belief the slaying may have occurred during rape or mayhem.

Bouchard insisted the special circumstances would allow a judge to sentence the suspects to life without parole if convicted, but he refused to give any more details about the case.

Fiorella, Delashmutt, and Casey all appeared for a detention hearing on that Tuesday, March 19. Their court files were sealed until after a hearing could be held to determine if they would be tried as adults.

Judge Michael Duffy immediately appointed lawyers Jennifer Fehlman and Kevin McReynolds for Casey and Fiorella. Delashmutt was to be represented by attorney Jeff Stein.

Fiorella refused to go into court that day when it was his turn to stand in front of the judge. He listened and watched from an adjacent room.

Meanwhile Elyse's family were determined to put the record straight about her.

They talked of the five-foot-seven-inch blue-eyed blond as a bright, intelligent girl who aspired to be an actress.

Elyse's uncle, Randy Rollins, proudly told one reporter how his niece could look at a dress and create a pattern without measuring or even laying out the various parts.

Rollins pointed out that his niece left the house the day she disappeared without taking anything— no clothes, no toothbrush, not even shoes. She left barefoot.

Randy Rollins and his wife Tina also insisted that their niece was a normal teenager, not a troubled youth. And they insisted that her murder was not drug related.

But the investigation into Elyse Pahler's death was only just beginning.

Thirteen

On the same week that Elyse's mutilated body was discovered by detectives, another child went missing, this time in the nearby city of Grover Beach.

Neighbors around the 100 block of Saratoga Avenue along with public-safety workers feared the worse when the parents of three-year-old Jessica Shelton reported her missing.

But because she was so much younger than Elyse, a huge search was immediately mounted. Police commanders estimated that some fifty people were involved in the search, and the child was found less than an hour later asleep under a blanket in the rear seat of her parents' car. She had slept through the search as her father drove the car around the neighborhood in a frantic effort to find her.

The Pahlers must have wished she had been their daughter.

* * *

By the beginning of the following week, investigators had reconfirmed what everyone really already knew; that the body discovered in that eucalyptus grove was Elyse Pahler.

Once again the news was blazed across the *Five Cities Times Press Recorder*, revealing that the "affable young high school student" died from "multiple stab wounds to her upper torso."

This time the newspaper corrected its earlier mistake that David Pahler was Elyse's stepfather. But it didn't really matter much to the heartbroken Pahler family.

The paper also reported that friends of the family had started a memorial fund to help the Pahlers.

Spokeswoman Patty Knotts said the family needed some assistance with funeral expenses, and any donation would be appreciated.

An account was even set up at the local Mid-State Bank, and readers were urged to make donations at any branch on account number 0125825721.

Local photographer Robert Dyer was well used to handling homicide inquiries, and he presumed that the sheriff's department would be releasing photos of the three suspects.

"But they didn't want to say anything about the names at that stage," recalled Dyer. "We couldn't even get any cooperation from the high school to get some photographs. It was a very difficult assignment."

Dyer and his colleagues would only actually manage to photograph the three defendants at their first court appearance later that month.

* * *

Journalists' attentions soon switched to other priorities when a rumor began circulating that there might have been some kind of satanic link with the death of Elyse Pahler.

"We heard just that satanic circumstances surrounded the killing. That was it," explained photographer Robert Dyer. "There was talk of a satanic ritual. We treated it as a rumor at first, and nobody took much notice. But we did try and press the sheriff for some reaction."

Sheriff Williams refused to be drawn into commenting on the claims despite repeated requests.

Then, just one week after the discovery of Elyse Pahler's mutilated body in that isolated eucalyptus grove, county prosecuting attorney Dodie Harman made a startling admission to local journalists.

"We're looking into issues, such as the possibility of satanism," she told one reporter. "If that's true, we'll have to research that."

Harman said that the investigation into Elyse's death was still ongoing and revealed that several people who knew suspects Fiorella, Delashmutt, and Casey had informed her that they were into devil worshiping.

Some of this startling new evidence came from Lopez High School student Shawn Whiteney, who knew two of the suspects. "Jacob told me that he worshiped Satan," said Whiteney.

Elyse's close friend Shannon Plotner was interviewed by reporters, and even told one journalist she knew the boys were into Satan. She also mentioned that the suspects had their own death metal band called "Hatred."

Immediately after the Satan links were revealed, rumors began circulating that there was an organized Satan cult on campus at Arroyo Grande High School.

Acting headmaster Mike Sears was shocked by the revelations, and insisted to reporters that such a group could not exist within the school.

However, at nearby Lopez High School, where Royce Casey was a pupil, school authorities arranged for extra counselors on campus for classmates who needed to talk to someone about what had happened.

Sheriff Ed Williams tried to play down the Satan links by insisting there was no evidence of a satanic ritual at the scene of Elyse's murder. But he conceded that the district attorney's office may have uncovered evidence from other sources.

Williams also tried to allay people's fears in the community that others might be in danger. "There has been no evidence that there is a current danger to other people. There also isn't any evidence that the suspects are part of a larger organization."

He refused to comment on whether there might be a link between Elyse's killing and the shooting death of a seventy-five-year-old woman by two youths, one of whom was Joe Fiorella's best friend Travis Williams.

The sheriff was bemused by the development, especially since he had not investigated any other cases in the county involving satanic rituals in the decade he'd been in charge.

It was clear that Royce Casey—who'd led investigators to Elyse's body—was the one feeling most remorseful about the killing.

On the Wednesday after the discovery of Elyse's body, Casey appeared briefly in court before Judge Michael Duffy with his parents and lawyer Kevin McReynolds. Duffy said that all three defendants should remain in custody at the county Juvenile Services Center.

In the hallway outside the courtroom, Casey's parents, Cecil and Rosalie, clutched each other's hands. "We grieve for Elyse's family," said Rosalie Casey. "We hope that everyone will pray for all the families involved."

The chill evening breeze was slightly warmed by candles and the memories of Elyse Pahler at a special memorial service held on Monday, March 25, at 7:00 P.M. in the Elm St. Park, in Arroyo Grande.

More than 300 people gathered with the Pahler family to remember and mourn the loss of the pretty teenager. Some came because they were her friends. Others wanted to comfort her family. And many came just to find solace as a community—to try and understand how something so horrible could have happened in a quiet backwater like Arroyo Grande.

Memories are a blessing, said Steve Carr, pastor at the Calvary Chapel, where the Pahlers regularly attended church.

"They remind you of what you've gained from her life. No one can take your memories from you," he told the crowd gathered in the park.

"God grieves over this tragedy. It should touch our hearts, and we should grieve over a senseless act like this."

Pastor Carr assured the family that their daughter, their granddaughter, their niece was with God. He said she may have died physically, but she lives again in heaven, and the family should take comfort in that.

Elyse's close friends Shannon and Angel were at the service, and Shannon told one reporter what Elyse meant to her.

"She was a happy person," Shannon said with tears rolling down her face. "And she could always make anyone laugh and make anyone happy."

Paul Sisemore, the youth pastor at the church, told the crowd he would always remember "that beautiful face" as Elyse spoke most assuredly about her faith. She was very firm in her convictions, he said. When he asked her if she knew Jesus, her reply was "Most definitely!"

During the service, Pastor Carr even made a passing reference to the three defendants when he told the crowd that "for two generations our society has been taught that there is no such thing as absolutes.

"But is there anyone who would deny that what was done to Elyse was absolutely wrong, was absolutely evil?" he asked rhetorically. "Be angry at sin; be angry at evil," he urged the crowd full of young people.

As the night grew darker, Pastor Carr drew the analogy between the candles, which began to glow brightly, and Elyse Pahler.

"Candles are a perfect picture of her life," he said. And he quoted King David, who said, "The spirit of life is the candle of the Lord."

The evening ended with a soulful, rhythmic arrangement of "Amazing Grace" sung by family friends Laura and Mark Folkrod.

Telegram-Tribune photographer Robert Dyer recalled that the service was very heartbreaking. "How can you fail to be sympathetic when something like this happens?"

But he also noticed a strange undertone to the service.

"There were a lot of Elyse's classmates there, and you couldn't help wondering how many of them knew what had really happened to her."

And Elyse's good friends Shannon and Angel admitted, "The service made us feel real sad, but we also felt angry because we were convinced that some of the kids there that night knew how Elyse had suffered."

Two days after the service—on March 27—Sheriff Ed Williams and his team of investigating detectives continued interviewing friends of both Elyse and the three suspects, Delashmutt, Fiorella, and Casey.

"Each student we talk with," said Detective Sergeant Steve Bolts, "seems to lead us on to a couple more interviews."

Both Bolts and his boss Williams were reluctant to reveal details of the case because their investigation was still ongoing. "We're still getting background," said Bolts.

They wanted to avoid rumors and hearsay clouding the investigation. They also wanted witnesses to tell what they knew firsthand rather than what they may have read in the newspapers or seen on TV.

They did not want to taint potential jurors if—as they hoped—the youths were eventually tried as adults.

"We have arrested who we think did it," Williams told reporters in San Luis Obispo. "We believe we had reasonable cause to do that. But they haven't been convicted yet."

Williams completely clamped down on any further discussion of the satanic connections. "Sometimes we can escalate things to a point where that's unwarranted," was his response to most reporters' inquiries.

But the sheriff could not deny that some form of satanic ritual *was* involved, although he continued to insist there was no evidence of an organized group of satanists at large in Arroyo Grande.

Detective Sergeant Bolts added, "If there was an organized group, then that might be a different situation; but there are no other arrests anticipated at this time.

"When we are confident all the witnesses who have information have been talked with," he said, "we may be able to disclose more. But that won't happen until at least next week."

Deputy District Attorney Dodie Harman admitted that the Satan elements involved in the case made it necessary for two prosecutors to be assigned to the case.

None of the prosecutors or detectives investigating the case would reveal whether drugs were directly involved in Elyse's death.

When asked whether the suspects were tested for them, Bolts replied with a terse, "No comment."

But all the lead investigators on the case said they fully understood the disbelief and anger of the community over Elyse's death.

"It was undoubtedly a horrific crime," one detective later explained. "Parents were understandably worried. Something like this should never have happened in a quiet place like Arroyo Grande."

On that same Wednesday, March 27, a hearing on the case in the San Luis Obispo juvenile court concluded after lawyer Dave Hurst was appointed to represent fifteen-year-old defendant Joe Fiorella.

With all three defendants now represented by legal counsel, the next court proceedings would be hearings beginning June 12 to determine if the three suspects were fit to stand trial as adults.

The case had already generated an intense interest within the San Luis Obispo County community, as indicated by the number of calls to local newspapers and TV stations, particularly from concerned families with school-age children.

In an unexpected move that same day, officials from the Juvenile Services Center ordered all members of the media to remain outside the facilities, and informed them they would not be permitted into the hearing.

A Probation Department representative said that juvenile court Judge Michael L. Duffy had interpreted and ruled that the California Welfare and Institutions Code Section 676 did not provide public access to all hearings of proceedings in which juveniles were accused of a capital crime.

That particular code section specified in part: "Except as provided by subdivision (b), members of the public shall be admitted, on the same basis as they may be admitted to trials in a court of criminal jurisdiction, to hearings concerning petitions filed persuant to Section 602."

Section 676 then goes on to list twenty-four specific crimes committed by juveniles in which the public shall be admitted to hearings and trials. Murder was on the list.

Subdivision (b) makes an exception for public access during the appearance of a minor victim of a rape and other such offenses, and section 602 simply defines a minor as anyone under eighteen years of age for purposes of jurisdiction by the juvenile court.

It was crystal clear that prosecutors were determined to throw the book at the boys despite their young ages.

But the judge was equally determined not to allow the

The memorial to Elyse Pahler that still stands at the spot where she was killed. *(Wensley Clarkson)*

The satanic lettering used by Jacob Delashmutt and his friend Joseph Fiorella on their school-books. *(Wensley Clarkson)*

Joseph Fiorella (left) and Jacob Delashmutt at a court appearance in the summer of 1996. *(Photo: Tom Parsons)*

Royce Casey in the San Luis Obispo court in the summer of 1996. *(Photo: Tom Parsons)*

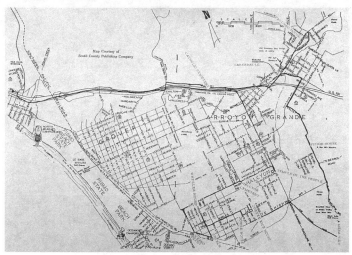

A map of Arroyo Grande. *(Wensley Clarkson)*

Elyse with her best friend Angel Katyryni. *(Shannon Plotner)*

Elyse in her favorite soccer shirt just a few months before her death. *(Shannon Plotner)*

Elyse and friend Shannon Plotner in a photo taken in a photo booth in Arroyo Grande shortly before her death. *(Shannon Plotner)*

Elyse in one of Angel's favorite photos.
(Shannon Plotner)

Elyse and her friend Shannon during a trip to the coast.
(Shannon Plotner)

Arroyo Grande High School. *(Wensley Clarkson)*

Elyse's best friends Shannon Plotner (left) and Angel Katyryni.
(Wensley Clarkson)

details of the case to be fully revealed until after the suspects' full hearing had got under way.

Not long after Elyse's body was discovered, the two teenagers who almost killed a woman with a baseball bat after breaking into her Arroyo Grande home were told they would stand trial for attempted murder.

The case of eighteen-year-old Matthew Schandel and his accomplice, seventeen-year-old Joshua Garner, was thrust into the spotlight because of ever growing local concern about teenage criminals in Arroyo Grande. Elyse's death was considered by many to be endemic of the crime wave sweeping through Arroyo Grande.

Fourteen

The Elyse Pahler murder case was growing increasingly difficult for the team of prosecutors and detectives working on it. Not only were they worried about the legal issues involved, but there was a growing concern about key witnesses in the case.

To no one's surprise, some of the victim's and suspects' classmates tried to recant evidence against the three youths. And others were showing signs of wavering.

While San Luis Obispo County prosecutors worked on the legal matters, Sheriff Ed Williams and his investigators continued probing for answers.

Williams' team had no doubts about the guilt of the three youths. Delashmutt and Fiorella appeared ruthless, coldhearted, and manipulative teenagers with absolutely no conscience. In their opinion they would stop at nothing—even sacrificing a young girl—to achieve their satanistic ambitions. They were convinced of their guilt and wanted to see them severely punished.

On the other hand, detectives were perplexed by Royce Casey. Those involved in the investigation had expressed concern about Casey's obvious weakness and his inability to make decisions for himself. While they believed that he had been the weak link in this killer threesome, they still believed he deserved to be punished just as severely, since he had kept the murder a secret for so long, and he was the oldest of the group.

In numerous meetings following his arrest, detectives saw Casey vacillate between anger, confusion, and help-lessness. One day Casey was full of remorse for every-thing that happened. The next day he wavered when he seemed to realize he was completely implicating him-self.

For much of the time, Casey completely failed to maintain his composure, but the detectives were very careful not to show any anger or any outward awareness of the ramifications of what had happened to Elyse.

Casey insisted throughout that he had been at a gro-cery store in the center of Arroyo Grande when Fiorella and Delashmutt bumped into him and persuaded him to go with them to meet Elyse Pahler. He said he played no part in planning the crime.

Fiorella and Delashmutt were told of Casey's com-ments, but refused to elaborate on what happened. They made it clear they were not happy with their onetime friend.

The San Luis Obispo juvenile courtroom was appropri-ated on May 4, 1996, for fifteen-year-old Joe Fiorella to face the world. It was an unusual scenario—the first appearance of a notorious alleged young killer—and deputies were understandably edgy and wary.

The big square room, inner core of the main courthouse, was packed. Reporters and photographers were given only a few minutes' grace before Fiorella was led in and the barred floor-to-ceiling door clanged shut behind him.

Dressed in a blue jumpsuit, feet thrust into thonged scuffs, Fiorella stood still for an instant, braced to meet the sharp slivers of camera lights. The young alleged murderer nodded distantly to his mom, Betsy Leo, and moved forward as his ankle chains clanked and scraped against the wooden flooring. Then he seated himself next to his attorney. He had found himself under the public spotlight during a brief hearing on new charges in the stalking, rape, torture, and killing of Elyse Pahler.

Fiorella looked even younger than his age and quite serene. His lawyer, Dave Hurst, waived a reading of the charges aloud. The two other suspects, Delashmutt and Casey, had been charged earlier because of their older ages and were allowed to listen and watch the complex proceedings from adjacent rooms.

Many people in the courtroom were shocked by the young alleged killer's behavior, unaware that he had refused to admit anything to detectives. To most, including the newspaper and television reporters who had rapidly assembled for the hearing, Fiorella was a cold-blooded killer. During the previous few weeks, stories about him and the other two youths had spread like wildfire across Arroyo Grande.

Now the teenager sat, straight-faced without a hint of emotion.

Judge Michael Duffy asked Fiorella if he understood the charges, and he answered, "Yeah." Duffy then set May 23 and 24 as the dates for a hearing requested by attorneys for all three defendants.

The lawyers for the two said their clients denied all the allegations, which now included—according to Deputy District Attorney Dan Bouchard—forming a musical band to glorify Satan and discussing the need for a human sacrifice to enhance their musical ability and earn a "ticket to hell."

Though he added a "gang" enhancement to the original charges, Bouchard insisted that he did not think there was widespread satanic worship in the south county.

Authorities also revealed they had seized Royce Casey's journal, which mentioned the killing, drug use, and sacrificing a virgin.

Casey's lawyer Kevin McReynolds said he'd ask for a special hearing to make prosecutors come up with some evidence of the satanic accusations. "It's called a prima facie hearing," explained McReynolds.

That hearing was scheduled before a so-called fitness hearing June 12 to see whether a judge believed the youths. If convicted, they could be rehabilitated in the juvenile court system. Prosecutors wanted the youths tried and convicted as adults.

McReynolds said he wanted the prima facie hearing to force the prosecution to present some evidence to substantiate its "baseless allegations." He also said a lot of the allegations were "grossly overstated, and some of them are flatly without any factual support whatsoever."

The defense lawyer said he thought many of the allegations were "intended to inflame public opinion."

Jeff Stein, who represented Delashmutt, also explained he would ask for the prima facie hearing. He told the court: "This is a terrible, tragic crime we're dealing with, but history recognizes there should be different treatment for younger defendants. I think life without parole is inappropriate for fourteen- and fifteen-year-olds."

Court documents filed at the time clearly stated: "The defendants formed a musical band to glorify Satan. To enhance their musical ability to worship Satan and thereby earn a 'ticket to hell.' They discussed the need for human sacrifices."

The filing further alleged that "to glorify Satan and commit the 'ultimate sin' against God, [they] selected a virgin . . . to sacrifice."

Deputy District Attorney Dan Bouchard, in the court documents, said the boys had stalked Elyse Pahler and aborted an earlier plan to kill her.

The documents also accused the boys of enlisting the help of Fiorella's friend Travis Williams, who was one of two suspects in the September 30 shooting death of seventy-five-year-old Mabel Agueda. Williams allegedly told authorities Delashmutt and Fiorella tried to get him to take part in what turned out to be an aborted attempt to kill Pahler before the night she died.

The documents claimed that Delashmutt, Fiorella, and Casey had a knife when they finally did take Pahler to an area on the Nipomo Mesa that they believed was an altar to Satan. The boys gave her drugs, the document clearly stated, to impair her ability to resist their "heinous, atrocious, and cruel" assault.

The documents also claimed one of the youths put a belt around Pahler's neck to hold her still while she was stabbed. Because the youths were accused of acting as a group, Deputy District Attorney Dan Bouchard included a gang "enhancement" that could increase the length of their sentence if they were convicted.

Until this point, all but the most relevant documents filed in the case had been sealed from the public because the defendants were juveniles. Authorities wanted the youths tried as adults, however, and a "fitness" hearing would eventually determine if that would occur.

But Deputy District Attorney Bouchard promised he would seal the records, if the judge granted him access. He also said he'd agree to closed-door meetings with the judge and the youth's lawyers to discuss them.

Fiorella got up at the end of the hearing, turned, and smiled in his mom's direction. As uniformed officers escorted him back out of the courtroom, he smirked across in the direction of the other two defendants. Delashmutt had his head held high. Casey was looking downward, hardly daring to look above the level of the floor.

The case's satanic elements drew TV, newspaper, and tabloid interest from all over the country.

Elyse's mother Lisanne even gave an interview to KNBC-TV during which she said the worst thing was thinking about the torture her daughter must have endured.

"Something is wrenched from you, a piece of your heart. That's what it feels like," she told the TV reporter, close to tears. "The pain, it's so great."

Tabloid TV shows vigorously pursued the Pahlers for interviews.

And even Sheriff Ed Williams got pulled into the nationwide interest when he issued a statement to reporters from national wire services, TV networks, and the tabloids, who had been flooding his department with inquiries ever since the satanic links to the case were revealed.

"The case is unusual not only because of its satanic nature but because homicides seldom happen here and because of the young age of the victim and the three defendants."

One of the sheriff's deputies, Rob Reid, breathlessly explained, "We've heard from CBS, NBC, ABC, Fox, and CNN."

Arroyo Grande was on the map for all the wrong reasons.

However, Williams still refused to disclose any further details about the investigation that led to the amended charges being filed.

"We don't ever want the defendants to say they didn't get a fair trial," he said. "We don't want to taint potential jurors."

Williams also insisted that no satanic material had been found at the scene of the murder. But he didn't discount that the accused youths might have found what they considered a "natural" altar. In other words, they did not have to alter the location in order to consider it an altar.

At Arroyo Grande High School many pupils were plainly too scared to talk about what they really knew about the case.

Investigators already believed that at least half a

dozen students knew about Elyse's death, because two of the suspects had been bragging about what they were alleged to have done.

"It was a nightmare scenario. Many of these kids were afraid to tell us what they knew because they thought they'd be implicated in the murder," explained one detective.

As Elyse's close friends Angel and Shannon later explained, "We were real mad at these people because they didn't want to get involved."

Shortly after returning to school, Angel heard that one of Royce Casey's friends had been saying that he knew all along that Elyse had been killed, but he'd been too frightened of the boys to tell anyone.

Angel confronted the boy at a friend's house and went ballistic.

"What is your problem? Why didn't you tell anyone?" yelled Angel.

"They'd have got me."

"What d'you mean?"

"They'd have killed me."

Angel walked away from the boy in disgust. She just couldn't understand why so many people were not telling the truth about what they knew of the case.

Fifteen

April 24, 1996, would have been Elyse Pahler's sixteenth birthday. Instead her family went to the mortuary in Arroyo Grande to say their farewells to the teenager.

Her grandmother Elyse Walter and mother Lisanne went ahead of the rest of the family and laid bright pink carnations all over her remains before everyone else arrived.

"It was something we had to do," Mrs. Walter later explained.

They all stood in the tiny mortuary in silent prayer for two minutes before looking at her for the last time.

After the family left the mortuary, Mrs. Walter drove out to the spot off Chamisal Road where her granddaughter died. She brought straw and silk flowers tied with a pink bow and laid them by a log. She placed a picture of a smiling Elyse in a glass screw-top jar and left a note:

"I love you Elyse and will always love you. Happy Birthday. Love Nana."

Elyse's funeral was held on that same warm and bright day. The sunshine glistened on the hoods of cars lining the one-lane roads that wandered through the San Luis Obispo cemetery.

Elyse's sisters and brother sat between David and Lisanne Pahler under a green canopy on a hill overlooking the neat roads and grassy verges. Relatives and friends of the Pahler family, along with dozens of Elyse's high school classmates, gathered around the graveside.

Listening to the minister talk of heaven and love and understanding, the Pahlers cried openly. Some of them felt guilty. Elyse's death hadn't seemed real until they saw the casket and flowers. They thought of all the times Elyse had sneaked out of the house at night. They kept wondering if it all could have been avoided. David Pahler was also angry at everything and everyone. He stared at the television cameramen and newspaper photographers who circled the graveside like vultures. He looked at her classmates and wondered how many of them knew something about his daughter's fate before the boys were arrested.

But what angered David Pahler the most was seeing the police standing nearby. He felt that they had never taken his fears about Elyse seriously enough.

The graveside service lasted only thirty minutes, but it seemed like an eternity to the Pahlers. After the service they drove back to their home in San Luis Obispo, where several friends and relatives were gathered.

"You're not supposed to live longer than your children," said one relative. "It's just not the way it should happen."

A few weeks later Lisanne Pahler called up her daughter's close friend Shannon Plotner.

"She was real nice. I was kinda confused at first as we'd not really spoken since the previous Christmas. I knew she'd felt that Angel and I were helping Elyse to hide out from her family," Shannon later explained.

"She thought Elyse had run away because the family were about to move to San Luis Obispo. Elyse's mom felt real bad about this."

Then Lisanne Pahler made a gesture of reconciliation toward her daughter's friend by insisting that Shannon should have some of the photos taken of her with Elyse and Angel.

A few days later the two met in a park near Shannon's home in Arroyo Grande, and Lisanne Pahler gave Shannon the photos and some mementos that Elyse had owned.

"It was a really good thing to do. I guess she was trying to say she'd been wrong about Angel and I. We really appreciated it," said Shannon later.

In custody, suspect Joe Fiorella assured his mom, Betsy Leo, that he'd broken off his close friendship with Travis Williams, also awaiting trial on murder charges following the shooting of an old lady in Arroyo Grande.

Under advice from his family and legal representatives, it was made crystal clear to Fiorella that his closeness to Williams could seriously affect the authorities' attitude toward him.

In any case, detectives believed that the Williams case also had certain "satanic elements" attached to it.

Betsy Leo even admitted to one local reporter that Williams had shown some interest in the occult when the teenager was staying as a long-term guest at her house, just a short distance from where Elyse Pahler was murdered.

Deputy prosecutors Dan Bouchard and Dodie Harman, both highly articulate attorneys, spent some weeks contemplating their next move in the Elyse Pahler murder case. Although the case was less than two months old, they were both already feeling the pressure. Reports from their staff had indicated the county's case against Casey, Delashmutt, and Fiorella had problems.

The issues complicating the case involved the police's investigation work; Bouchard and Harman knew the sheriff's detectives had worked hard. But the problems stemmed from the fact that many of the potential witnesses were teenage schoolchildren. The availability and willingness of these key witnesses was crucial, and many of them had started to recant their earlier statements. Many were also tainted by the newspaper and television reports of the case, not to mention the rumors that were flying around Arroyo Grande at an alarming rate.

Sitting alone in their office, Bouchard and Harman carefully considered their options. Should they continue to pursue a first-degree murder charge against the boys and risk losing it because of their age and the lack of cooperation from Fiorella and Delashmutt? Or should they reduce the charges, weather the public outcry, and hope that they could secure heavy prison sentences when the case actually came to trial?

Both attorneys were worried not only about the public's reaction to the reduction of charges, but also about the reaction of the detectives to the case.

Like most murder cases where arrests have been made, the detectives involved in this case were more confident than the prosecutors.

Sheriff Williams and his detectives had been surprised and angered during a meeting with the prosecutors when they were informed there was a possibility the charges might be reduced to take into account the youths' ages. They had immediately pushed Bouchard and Harman to proceed with first-degree murder charges.

The problem was compounded by the inconsistency of the witnesses' testimony. It was one thing to believe someone had committed a crime, but another thing to convince a jury beyond a reasonable doubt.

The prosecutors knew they needed Fiorella and Delashmutt to confess; otherwise they could be facing an uphill struggle.

The prosecutors reiterated that the boys' lawyers were focusing their attention on trying to prevent the county attorneys from having the youths tried as adults.

As one investigator pointed out, "It was a difficult situation. We believed we had more than enough evidence to complete a successful prosecution, but no one was quite sure what charges the boys should ultimately face."

Betsy Leo somehow still found comfort in the tatty old photographs she continued to carry in a worn white envelope at all times. Every so often she'd find herself at home on her own and simply spread the stack of pictures across a table, looking hard at the dimpled face of the same boy smiling in each shot.

"I look at these pictures—my favorite is this one of him in his Little League uniform—and I find myself asking over and over, how does a child go from this," the forty-seven-year-old mom said haltingly, "to a shackled person staring back at me from the front page."

Leo's son, Joe Fiorella, had grown into what prosecutors alleged was one of the ringleaders in the gruesome murder of Elyse Pahler.

For Betsy Leo the suffering could never be as bad as that of David and Lisanne Pahler, but it was still immensely painful.

Just two days after Fiorella's arrest, the divorced mother of two sons was fired from her job.

"I don't want to say where I worked, but I will say I was told I wasn't doing the job, after I was given a raise for doing a good job."

Leo was closing the shop where she worked when her business partner told her the police were looking for her son that bleak Thursday night in March, 1996.

Leo had actually been expecting the police to call at the family home to ask questions about his best friend, Travis Williams, who'd been arrested months earlier in connection with the shooting of an Arroyo Grande grandmother in her own home.

Williams had been a guest in Leo's home for quite some time. But Betsy Leo insisted that both boys were well behaved and polite—never violent.

When detectives came to her house March 14 to question and then arrest her son on suspicion of murder, Leo said she went into shock. "I felt like I'd gotten to the edge of losing my sanity."

In the weeks following Fiorella's arrest, Leo kept trying to come to terms with what was happening.

"I never got to the point where I blamed myself, because playing the blaming game is a trap," she later explained. "It would be much easier to deal with this psychologically and emotionally if I could blame something, even myself, but there are too many factors involved."

Leo admitted she had always been open with both her boys about religion and her moral and ethical values.

And she insisted that children were committing murder because they are taught society no longer values life, whether through music, abortion, war, or the way murder is glorified in the media.

But she believed that her son Joseph was definitely a candidate for rehabilitation despite the accusations that had been made against him.

"I have as many questions as the community has: What's going on? I can't pinpoint what happened. Why can't we explore the causes through rehabilitation? At this point, if he's convicted of everything, he won't be eligible for parole until he's forty," she said.

"In some ways, it would be much easier for him to be dead than to keep going to see him behind bars in shackles and not being able to help. But of course I'm glad he's not dead. But I've lost my son, too."

Leo was equally emotionally upset about Elyse Pahler's family.

"There are no words to express my sorrow at the grief they are going through. I envision a time when we can all come together with a mediator and bare our hearts, and find it in our hearts to forgive," explained Leo, referring to the Pahlers and the families of the other boys accused in the killing.

She was even in favor of the eventual trials being televised. "I think it would be cathartic healing for the community."

Leo was allowed to visit her son for just two hours a month. Fiorella's father and older brother also managed a visit each month.

"There's this conflict," Leo said. "First there's the shock of hearing or reading about the horrible things that happened to a girl in our community, and then the shock of being the parent of a child accused of such a thing."

With her eyes brimming with tears, Leo added, "There are times when I want to tell him, like any mother would, that everything's going to be OK and it's time to go home now. But I can't take him home and make everything all right. It's out of my control."

Sixteen

News of Elyse Pahler's murder and the satanic links to the case were appearing in virtually every newspaper across the country by the beginning of May, 1996.

Many publications initially ran the story based on an Associated Press news agency piece circulated on May 5, which was headlined TEENAGERS CHARGED IN GIRL'S RITUAL SACRIFICE.

The story reported that Elyse Pahler was killed as "a sacrifice to Satan" in what represented a "ticket to hell." It also revealed that the three teenagers were charged with feeding her drugs, raping her, and cinching a belt around her neck to make it easier to stab her.

Any belief on the part of the prosecutors and the police that the satanic elements of the case could be kept under wraps had been completely blown wide open.

Now not only did the police department have to contend with a nonstop barrage of press inquiries, but doz-

ens of Satan followers were calling at all times of the
day and night asking obscure questions about the more
grisly details of the case.

"The weird thing was that these people would call up
as if it were perfectly normal to contact us with bizarre
questions about Elyse's murder. I was sickened by it,"
explained one Arroyo Grande officer.

On the Internet, one bright spark set up a section up-
dating devil worshipers on the progress of the case.

On May 23, 1996, attorneys for Delashmutt and Fiorella
filed a motion asking Judge Michael Duffy to dismiss
"special circumstances," such as torture and rape, that
had been added to the charges facing the suspects in the
killing of Elyse Pahler.

Chris Casciola, of Casciola and Stein, the firm representing Delashmutt, and Dave Hurst, Fiorella's lawyer,
claimed that because the crime occurred when their clients were under sixteen, special circumstances did not
apply. Such circumstances raised the potential punishment from life in prison to life in prison without possibility of parole.

The penal code, said Casciola, laid out the potential
punishment for youths from sixteen to eighteen, but did
not clearly state what happened to people under that age.

Before going into the hearing, Casciola explained,
"We're asking the judge to rule on this ambiguity because there's nothing said about appropriate punishment
for a juvenile under sixteen. We're saying our clients
can't be exposed to the possibility of life in prison without possibility of parole."

The other suspect, Royce Casey, was sixteen when

Elyse died from multiple stab wounds in July, 1995.

Assistant District Attorney Dan Bouchard admitted he thought this was the first time the "under sixteen" issue had been raised in the state. He said he was intending to work with the Attorney General's Office on researching a response to the defendant's motion.

Whichever way Judge Duffy eventually ruled could in any case be appealed by either side.

Neither Casciola nor Bouchard would discuss specifics of the case, noting a "gag order" Duffy had imposed on all involved.

That order in effect banned anyone involved in the case from speaking publicly about it until the boys actually went to trial.

Larry Reiner, executive officer of the county Superior Court, said that Judge Duffy was not expected to continue the hearing on the defense lawyers' most recent motion until June 12, when a hearing was also scheduled to determine whether the three youths were fit for rehabilitation in the juvenile court system. Prosecutors were still insisting they be tried as adults.

Reiner explained that the prima facie hearing—a hearing where prosecutors must show they have sufficient evidence to continue the case—would not be held until those June 12 proceedings.

While Joe Fiorella and Jacob Delashmutt continued to refuse to cooperate with investigators, those who knew Royce Casey were insisting that while it was no surprise that he was in trouble, the gravity of his problems were another matter.

To most people, Casey was a rascal, not a cold-blooded killer. He was a teenager with an abundance of energy, but little guidance or motivation. He had been suspended from high school many times for disciplinary problems. But he had no juvenile record and rarely displayed any propensity for violence.

Casey was a likable, proud youth with an easy smile and a desire to be known as a ladies' man. He also was very lonely.

It was clear to everyone—counselors, teachers, and police—that Casey had the intellectual and social skills to succeed. He just didn't have the desire.

But for Casey, school was social, not educational. When things didn't go right, he would leave, often going to a friend's house to do drugs or drink. And that was how he got pulled into the lives of Travis Williams, Jacob Delashmutt, and Joe Fiorella.

On June 19, 1996, juvenile court Judge Michael Duffy threw out the special circumstance charges of rape, torture, and stalking against the two youngest defendants, fifteen-year-old Fiorella and sixteen-year-old Delashmutt. He ruled that the youths—aged fourteen and fifteen at the time of the murder—were too young to be charged with special circumstances.

However, seventeen-year-old Royce Casey could still face life without the possibility of parole if convicted. The special circumstances charges apply to defendants sixteen or older and, if proven, add to the severity of their sentence. State law allowed those sixteen or older to be given life without parole or—for those eighteen or older—to face the death penalty. Juveniles cannot be executed in California.

Fiorella's attorney Dave Hurst and Delashmutt lawyer Jeff Stein successfully argued there would be no consequence for the special circumstance charges, and therefore they should be dismissed.

But evidence of the special circumstances charges could still be presented at a fitness hearing, where Duffy would rule whether the boys would be tried in juvenile or adult court.

Prosecutor Dodie Harman acknowledged that she and fellow prosecutor Dan Bouchard faced an uphill battle to reintroduce the special circumstance charges.

Elyse's family, including her mother and father, her grandmother, and her aunt and uncle, crowded into the courtroom along with parents and family supporters of the three suspects.

After the hearing, the Pahler family issued a written statement, which said in part:

> *"The Pahlers know their daughter is with their Lord, Jesus Christ. They are praying for the perpetrators that they will receive God's forgiveness and mercy, but at the same time for justice and righteousness to prevail. They are convinced that through God's grace something good will come out of this tragedy."*

Seventeen

Elyse Pahler's parents David and Lisanne suffered the kind of mental torture only those who have lost loved ones in similar circumstances would appreciate.

Their every waking moment was filled with thoughts of Elyse and the pain and suffering she must have endured on that dreadful night of July 22, 1995.

While the notes and calls of sympathy continued to flood in, nothing was going to bring their daughter back, and they were finding it extremely hard to come to terms with what had happened.

Some days they just cried and cried. Other days they got angry about the system that had allowed their daughter to fall victim to a set of circumstances they believed was not beyond their control.

One of the main thrusts of their bitterness was aimed toward the musical groups that belonged to the so-called death metal rock craze, which had swept through Arroyo

Grande High School and many other schools throughout the nation over the previous few years.

The Pahlers were convinced that the violence-drenched lyrics that accompanied many of the songs by groups such as Slayer inspired the three youths to kill their daughter.

So exactly one year after Elyse Marie Pahler slipped away from their home—the same night investigators believed she was repeatedly stabbed to death in the eucalyptus grove—David and Lisanne Pahler filed a lawsuit against Slayer at the San Luis Obispo County Superior Court.

They were not legally bound to file until a year after Elyse's body had been found, but felt it was important to file on the first anniversary of her disappearance.

The band and its record company, American Recordings, should be held responsible, according to the suit, because Slayer's lyrics incite listeners to "take violent, destructive action toward teenage females."

The suit also named the three accused youths, and alleged their parents or guardians should be held responsible in civil court. It stated: "The parents breached their duties by failing to exercise reasonable supervision and control over their sons, who were 15, 15 and 17 years old respectively, at the time of Elyse's murder."

The suit did not specify the amount of money being sought, although it did ask for punitive damages.

"The defendants' parents knew or should have known of their tendencies and habits toward satanism and violence," the suit alleged.

David Pahler insisted that he and his wife wanted the

lawsuit to bring public attention to the type of music accessible to kids.

"This is filth," he said. "No wonder we have kids out there murdering. People don't know what's going on out there. Satan worship is a nationwide organization. It's underground, but it's pretty big in this country."

Since news of his daughter's appalling killing had spread across the country, Pahler had started receiving information from many different sources regarding the satanic movement. It was those contacts who encouraged him to file the lawsuit.

One of Pahler's primary objectives in filing the lawsuit was to bring the issue to the attention of people across the nation.

"It is just now getting attention. It is just now coming to the surface on all levels."

He told reporters he intended to push for legislation that would put certain music off-limits to youths, much as pornographic material is restricted.

"They can get ahold of Slayer music talking about murder and sacrificing," added Pahler. "You tell me where you draw the line.

"I don't think minors should be allowed to be exposed to this sort of thing. They're not allowed to be exposed to a lot of [other] things."

Slayer had recorded several albums and CDs in the decade-plus of its existence, including a 1985 recording titled *Hell Awaits*.

Band members Tom Araya, Kerry King, and Jeff Hanneman were named in the suit.

David Pahler had been stunned when he heard one

song from the album, "Necrophiliac," which included lyrics about a "virgin child" who would "rot in hell."

But it was the lyrics in another song entitled "Kill Again" that completely and utterly convinced Pahler to bring action against Slayer:

> *"Trapped in mortal solitude, lift the gleaming blade. Slice her flesh to shreds, watch the blood flow free."*

Pahler was also disgusted by the contents of the promotional jacket sold with the CDs by Slayer.

The *Divine Intervention* CD featured a collage of photographs depicting people who had died for Satan. Another photo showed a young man with the word "Slayer" carved in his arm with blood running from the wounds.

And as if to taunt crusaders like David Pahler, the promotional material also featured newspaper headlines announcing the failure of lawsuits similar to the one that the Pahlers had filed.

Slayer's manager, Rick Sales, said it was the first lawsuit ever filed against the band.

"I don't think that's held water in any previous attempts," Sales said of similar lawsuits against other recording groups.

Earlier lawsuits against artists such as Ozzy Osbourne and Judas Priest failed to convince judges or juries of links between lyrics and someone's actions, concurred one expert in First Amendment litigation.

The lawsuits in those cases involved suicides that surviving family members alleged were inspired by the lyrics of the musicians.

One litigation expert explained, "We've repeatedly seen attempts to punish musicians and rock 'n' roll groups . . . for various messages and various depictions of violence.

"But invariably the cases fail because the First Amendment protects speech that doesn't incite someone to commit violence against a specific person or group.

"The point is, there's all kinds of messages in the Bible, in music, in movies, which can be construed . . . as having a general message of violence.

"When you move away from that . . . to generalized speech, the law is you cannot hold people liable . . ."

In a Missouri murder case, however, a psychiatrist testified that the defendant "suffered from an induced psychosis" caused by obsessively listening to lyrics advocating violence and referring to hell.

An appellate court that upheld a first-degree murder conviction in the case, however, noted that "perhaps [the jury] doubted the influence of music on the mind, realizing that under modern history's most evil society, Wagner's 'Ride of the Valkyrie' preceded Der Führer's speeches . . . and inmates of the death camps, spared because of their musical abilities, played Hady and Mozart as their compatriots marched past them toward the gas chambers."

But David Pahler had absolutely no doubt of the music's influence on the minds of young people.

"These young kids don't get to grow up and realize their earliest dreams. We're trying to put a stop to all this. Adolescents, they cannot get pornography and a lot of things out there that would have an effect on these kids. . . . We say as a society, these are the things that we don't want them exposed to. I believe in freedom of speech, but this goes a bit too far.''

Pahler admitted he had no idea if the lawsuit would be successful. He simply felt driven to file an action in the hope that it might one day help prevent another tragedy from occurring.

Eighteen

The shrub land and grass trails leading to the over-hanging eucalyptus grove had grown to such an extent, it was hard to imagine the number of investigators and their vehicles who'd trampled through the overgrowth just three months earlier.

But the area immediately surrounding the spot where Elyse Pahler was so cruelly murdered exhibited a smooth, worn pattern where numerous mourners had stood to pay their respects—and the curious questioned what really happened that windy summer's night the previous year.

The memorial site had become somewhat serene. A photograph of pretty fifteen-year-old blond freshman Elyse was fastened to one of the fallen logs at the spot where she met her terrible death. Mementos of flowers, ribbons, homemade wreaths, and a small teddy bear were laid out nearby.

Around the unofficial memorial stood a tall, spindly eucalyptus tree adorned with barren wispy branches that looked like they had survived some previous forest fire. At night they may have created the image of a dark, eerie altar to Satan, as prosecutors charged.

The strangest thing about the location of Elyse's death—just thirty yards from the roadway of Chamisal Lane—was its close proximity to people's homes. A resident's four-rail corral fence lay just a few feet from the death scene. A house sat no more than fifty yards away behind that fence.

Beyond that lay the home of one of the accused youths, Joe Fiorella, nestling among the eucalyptus trees less than a quarter of a mile from where Elyse was killed. The urge to go back to the scene of her death was, say prosecutors, irresistible.

Even if the place was at one time an altar to Satan in the minds of the accused killers as prosecutors allege, subsequent visitors had made an obvious effort to create something just the opposite.

The location for the "ultimate sin against God," as charged in the court documents, had been transformed into a place that recognized God, as observed by the inscriptions on gifts and notes left to honor the victim.

Around this time, suspect Royce Casey agreed to take a polygraph test for his attorney, Kevin McReynolds. It was a controversial move by the lawyer, who was only too aware of the way in which his client had virtually been tried and convicted in the media before any trial could get under way.

But McReynolds believed Casey when he pleaded

with the attorney that he had not taken part in the sexual side of the assault on Elyse Pahler. He was desperate to prove that to the court.

Casey was understandably nervous about taking the polygraph at the Juvenile Services Center. He went through a brief pretest interview, during which he was told the nature of the questions he would be asked during the test.

Then two pneumotubes were placed on his upper and lower chest. Next followed a blood pressure cuff before wires were linked to two of his fingertips to measure his eventual perspiration during questioning. The theory behind polygraphs is that they measure the fear of detection in a subject. Experts claim that when a subject lies, his or her body goes into "flight mode," which is picked up on the graph linked to those wires.

Over the following hour and a half, Casey took at least three separate tests, during which he was asked the same set of questions. Between each test the heavily perspiring teenager was given a breather so that his blood pressure did not go too high. The polygraph machine measured Casey's temperature, blood pressure, perspiration, and breathing throughout the questioning.

The specific responses of Casey to the polygraph cannot be revealed for legal reasons. But when it came to the question of him sexually assaulting Elyse, he emphatically denied this, and the polygraph showed him to be telling the truth.

In San Luis Obispo criminal court on Wednesday, June 26, Casey's attorney McReynolds asked the court to admit into evidence the lie detector test, which would indicate his client did not sexually abuse the girl.

Kevin McReynolds, representing Casey, said, "Mr.

Casey in no way was involved in any kind of sexual misconduct in any way.''

The lawyer argued that a current polygraph test should be considered scientific evidence. ''It is relatively as good if not better than scientific evidence admitted in courts today.''

He also intimated that it could be considered better than eyewitness testimony in some cases.

McReynolds said that based on the results of the lie detector test, there was only a ''0.01 percent chance that Casey was being untruthful about any sexual misconduct.''

However, prosecutors complained that they would need time to call in nationally recognized experts to analyze the procedures and results of the polygraph test.

Prosecutor Dodie Harman also suggested to the court that if by sexual misconduct McReynolds was ''referring to rape, it is irrelevant in a fitness hearing.''

Harman also pointed out that the prosecution only has to show that the ''degree of criminal sophistication exhibited'' or ''the circumstances and gravity of the offense alleged'' are such that the juvenile court judge will find minors are ''not fit and proper'' subjects to be dealt with under juvenile court law.

And in the interests of ''fairness'' in allowing the test into the proceedings, McReynolds even seemed willing to concede some points to the prosecution. The lawyer admitted in his argument that Casey's answers to some questions in the lie detector test showed that his client took part in ''some pretty horrible things.''

McReynolds also made the point that the favorable polygraph results would dispute the prosecution's evidence against Casey in the fitness hearing and in a separate "probable cause" hearing. However Prosecutor Bouchard went on to say that it was "not simply a matter of hiring a good technician, getting good equipment, and finding good, clean, readable charts."

Judge Duffy said he would take the motion and the legal briefs under submission and would notify them of his decision in writing.

After the hearing, none of the court officials were willing to estimate how long it would take Duffy to make his decision. And no one speculated on the outcome.

In another issue, Bouchard asked the court to open any files the Mariposa Community Recovery Center might have on any of the accused and the victim. Those drug-related records are sealed and kept confidential by federal law.

Stories had been circulating since the discovery of Elyse's body that one or more of the accused teenagers had met their victim while participating in the rehabilitation program at the center. In fact, Elyse and Delashmutt had definitely encountered each other.

Bouchard acknowledged that he did not know if such a relationship had existed through the center. The purpose of his motion to have the files opened was an attempt to discover if there was any relevant information contained in them.

In August, 1996, the San Luis Obispo County Probation Service argued at a juvenile court hearing that all three suspects should be moved to the county jail in San Luis Obispo.

County attorney Mary A. Toepke said that eighteen-year-old Casey was now an adult and the other two defendants, sixteen-year-old Fiorella and sixteen-year-old Delashmutt, should be moved because they were a detriment to other teenage prisoners.

But the attorneys for all three claimed their clients were well behaved and posed no threat to the public, and therefore should remain at the juvenile hall.

At the hearing courtroom audiences got a first glimpse of all three prisoners, each in shackles and wearing blue jumpsuits, together for the first time since their first juvenile court appearance in March.

Seeing no cameras in the courtroom, Kevin McReynolds motioned for Casey, standing in an adjacent waiting room, to take a seat next to him, where he sat throughout the proceedings. Casey's hair was in a ponytail.

Previously, only Fiorella had taken a seat in court because he wanted to be closer to his mother, who was sitting in the audience. But this time Fiorella stayed in an adjoining room.

Meanwhile Delashmutt had had his blond ponytail sheared to a crew cut, which was far darker since his incarceration the previous March.

Probation officer James Salio testified that the boys should be moved to the jail because it had been determined that they would be treated as adults.

Salio also mentioned a spitting incident between Delashmutt and Casey. The probation officer said that Casey was now being threatened by his onetime friend.

There was also testimony that other teens in the juvenile hall were uncomfortable in the presence of the defendants, either because they knew the victim or because they were horrified by the accusations.

At least one prisoner routinely asked to be locked in his cell rather than interact with the defendants, said Salio.

County attorney Toepke also argued that the youths could be a negative influence on teens who did communicate with them.

But defense attorneys said it was irrelevant how other prisoners felt about who they were housed with.

McReynolds pointed out that Casey was a model prisoner, who had accumulated high point totals awarded for good behavior.

Fiorella's attorney, Dave Hurst, said his client had neither tried to escape nor caused any problems with prisoners or guards—a claim not all juvenile prisoners could make.

And except for his soured relationship with Casey, Delashmutt's attorney claimed he had caused no problems at Juvenile Hall, either.

After hearing all the evidence, Judge Michael Duffy said he would reissue a written ruling about whether the three youths should be transferred at a future date.

The complicated aspects of prosecuting three teenagers for murder were only just beginning.

Nineteen

The Pahlers' mailbox at their new home in San Luis Obispo continued to be filled each and every morning with dozens of letters of sympathy even several months after their beloved daughter's death.

But in the summer of 1996 they received a letter that cruelly reminded them of the evil forces at work in our society. It was the first in a series of postcards from a satanist writing to their deceased daughter.

The family was horrified but powerless to stop the disturbing mail, which consisted of appalling references to Elyse from the sick and twisted mind of a self-confessed devil worshiper.

The letters also indicated that the man was living in the Arroyo Grande area, and had been a regular visitor to the site where Elyse was slain.

"They were awful. Elyse's death caused so much

heartache yet we then had to contend with this sort of thing," her grandmother later explained.

The family handed the letters over to the police department, but they could do little about them, since the writer was not actually breaking any laws.

"The worst thing about it was that these letters were addressed to my dead granddaughter, as if we wouldn't be upset by their contents. They were the work of a very sick and twisted mind," added Elyse Walter.

The matriarchal figure of Elyse Pahler's grandmother, Elyse Neilson Walter, cast a powerful shadow over all aspects of the case in the months following the teenager's murder.

In many ways she had become the unofficial spokeswoman for the family. She had felt an enormous bond with Elyse. They had very similar characters, and Mrs. Walter had absolutely no doubt Elyse would have been an extremely successful adult if her life had not been so cruelly cut short.

Mrs. Walter was particularly outspoken when it came to discussing what sort of punishment should face the three youths charged with killing her granddaughter.

"In the state of Texas they execute fifteen-year-olds for murder. I think they should do the same thing here in California."

Mrs. Walter was deeply concerned about the way that Elyse's parents continued to struggle to come to terms with their daughter's death.

"Every time David reads anything in the newspapers or on the television, he freaks out. It's so hard for them to cope. I'm just tryin' to give them a helping hand."

And, somewhat inevitably, the sleazier elements continued to pick up on the nastier aspects of the case.

One crime detective magazine published a sensational report describing in detail how the teenagers allegedly killed Elyse to earn themselves "a ticket to hell."

Highly salacious reports such as these were deeply disturbing to the Pahlers.

"They made Elyse's death even more difficult to handle, and they kept implying things about her that just weren't true," explained her grandmother.

"They also encouraged every Satan creep in the country to try and contact us, and blacken the name of my beloved granddaughter."

Mrs. Walter was also instrumental in setting up a special foundation in Elyse's name shortly after her death.

However, the family found they were extremely restricted from doing anything for the foundation at first because of the judge's gagging order that effectively prevented them from talking about the case.

It specified that, "No witness, or person subpoenaed as a witness shall make or authorize for public dissemination the making of an extra judicial statement concerning the case. No person shall authorize or realize any documents that are evidence in connection with the case . . ."

As one lawyer involved in the case explained, "I cannot in good faith allow my clients to talk publicly about the case at this moment. It would be contempt of court. The judge has told us all this in chambers."

David Pahler and his mother-in-law even met officials at the district attorney's office to find out what they could and could not do in relation to public statements and official business on behalf of the Elyse Foundation.

It was a classic example of David Pahler's vulnerability at the time and how he needed Elyse Walter with him for the meeting.

"He said to me, 'Mom, can you be there with me' and I naturally said 'yes,' " Walter later explained.

There was a certain tension between the Pahler family and the police as they still felt the police had not taken Elyse's disappearance seriously enough. Forensic experts suggested that the teenager was still alive when her assailants left her in the eucalyptus grove—implying that if an immediate search had been mounted of the area, then she might have been found alive.

However, the sad truth was that Elyse stood no chance of survival beyond a few minutes after that brutal, multiple assault.

The meeting between the family and the district attorney plus some other officials included the district attorney's investigator Doug Odom, who had played a pivotal role in the office's inquiries since the arrest of Delashmutt, Fiorella, and Casey.

Grandmother Elyse Walter was very impressed by Odom. "The minute you meet him, you know you're dealing with a real gentleman, not some country bumpkin," she explained.

But the family felt extremely frustrated not being able to organize the Elyse Foundation. Investigators feared that any mention of her name might taint any eventual juries in the court cases involving the three suspects.

Besides the regular media interest in the case, Hollywood came calling when it became clear that the Elyse Pahler story had certain dramatic elements that could be easily converted into a TV movie of the week.

At first the family was too upset to cope with the approaches, but toward the end of 1996, the family decided they would meet up with representatives of all the major networks to see what sort of offers were on the table.

"Not a week goes by without some offer or other for the rights to Elyse's story," explained Mrs. Walter.

But once again the judge's gag order proved a difficult hurdle because none of the networks wanted to commit without knowing more of the gory details. And, for the moment, the full story of what really happened that night remained locked in the DA's office. The statements taken in the case were out of bounds to the public while deals were being struck between lawyers representing the three youths and prosecutors.

The other frustration for the family at this time was that their legal suit against the Slayer death metal band was effectively in limbo because they could not get at any of those same statements that might incriminate the band in the death of Elyse.

The Pahler family lawyer, Allan Hutkin, found himself fielding most of the media inquiries, but his hands were also effectively tied by the judge's gag order.

Elyse's grandmother and the rest of the family were also very concerned by what they saw as an unnecessary shadow being cast over the good name of Elyse.

"Elyse wasn't sleazy," she explained. "She was a top-notch young woman and had her life carefully planned out. She knew exactly what she wanted to do, unlike the youths accused of her murder. They had no idea of what the future held for them. But they had murder on their hands."

Mrs. Walter saw her granddaughter's killing as the tip

of the iceberg as far as teenage crime was concerned.

"It's unbelievable these days. It's getting worse and worse. In my day when a kid didn't like the teacher, they would put gum on their seat. Now they put poison in their Coca-Cola and try to kill them."

Mrs. Walter hoped that eventually the foundation in her daughter's name "might actually be able to do something."

She added, "We are looking forward to the trial. But we just wait from one day to the next to see what will happen."

On Friday, August 30, 1996, Judge Michael Duffy ordered that the three suspects be transferred from the Juvenile Services Center to the county jail, where they would await arraignment in the Superior Court on the charges they faced.

The three teenagers were to be held under maximum-security conditions in the tough county jail because of a state law governing minors housed in jails in close proximity to arrestees from the general population.

In the county jail the three youths found themselves subjected to the same rules that governed all other prisoners. Those rules specified that they would be allowed three hours a week, under guard escort, for exercise outside their cells. Plus, because they were minors, they would be isolated from the others in the jail at all times.

The suspects' families immediately complained that three hours was not a long enough time for their sons to be out of their cells. Some members of the families were also upset because they could only communicate

with the boys during visits via a telephone through a
slab of reinforced glass.

At the Juvenile Services Center, the families had been
allowed face-to-face contact. Jail officials pointed out
that the rules applied to all prisoners to ensure the prisoners' safety as well as the safety of those who worked
there.

The order by Judge Duffy to move the trio followed
a recommendation by the County Probation Department
to separate them from others at the juvenile center.

Intriguingly, Royce Casey's attorney Kevin McReynolds referred in court to his client as a "peer leader"
among those housed at JSC. Yet others close to the case
contended that Casey spent most of his time in his room
away from the others because of fear of reprisals.

Attorneys for each of the other defendants echoed Mc-
Reynolds' remarks by claiming that "there have been
absolutely no problems" concerning the boys, and that
"they are being very good prisoners" at the juvenile
center.

The lawyers also argued that there had been "sub-
stantial evidence" to find out if the juveniles were "a
danger to the public." The lawyers believed that the
Probation Department only wanted their clients removed
from the Juvenile Services Center for convenience to the
department's operations.

Walking into the county jail at San Luis Obispo was
exactly like walking into a room lined with animal
cages. All prisoners had a full view of any other prisoner
in his cell.

Delashmutt, Fiorella, and Casey heard arguments and

threats being hollered in their direction much of the time.

It was impossible not to hear the taunts of other inmates. The three youths knew they had to be careful not to get one of the prisoners running off his mouth at them. That meant being friendly and conversing with them about any subject they might want to discuss, but that was only through bars. No face-to-face contact would be allowed.

All day inside the county jail, from breakfast to supper time, was broken up by guards. Each prisoner's door was opened onto the tier one at a time. Then inmates could shower, sweep out their cell, and pace the tier in front of the cells of others.

Many inmates would hang around the boys' cells, smiling and watching. Some would make obscene suggestions. Some would hound them because they were fresh, young meat. They'd harass the youths, and there was absolutely nothing they could do about it.

The closest the boys could come to adjusting to the underlining threat of life inside the county jail was to will themselves to sleep all day through all the many jail disturbances. After each meal, they would curl up, pull their blankets over themselves, put their pillows over their ears, and try to sleep.

When the lights would go out at night, they would lie there, often awake for hours because of all that middle-of-the-day sleeping. Staying up much of the night had its own advantages. The distractions had disappeared. The freaks' faces were not in front of them anymore.

But during that period, they couldn't read or write or even listen to a radio. All they could hear was the staff making their rounds. They heard keys and chains rattling and the sounds of other prisoners sleeping.

Each of the boys reacted differently. Casey was afraid of the other inmates and his codefendants. He believed his only chance of survival was to stay locked up in that cell.

Fiorella was the youngest, and in many ways the most vulnerable. He was overawed by the sheer size of the county jail and the inmates, many of whom were old enough to be his grandfather. He was bewildered and slightly apprehensive.

Delashmutt remained the cocky, confident one. He seemed to show no fear about life inside the county jail. He also made sure that Casey knew he was well aware of how Casey had gone to the authorities to tell them what had happened to Elyse Pahler.

In September, 1996, Casey's newly appointed lawyer asked the judge to reconsider allowing her client to give up his right to be prosecuted in a juvenile court.

The attorney, Theresa Klein, hadn't represented Casey when he and his two codefendants agreed to be prosecuted as adults and relinquished their rights to a hearing in juvenile court.

Klein argued that such a move was legally improper.

The request, in the form of a writ to Judge Duffy, declared that the court action was in error. The lawyer then asked the judge to review the process that led to his ruling with regard to any illegalities and inequities that may have occurred.

But prosecutors felt otherwise. Noted Deputy District Attorney Dan Bouchard outside the courtroom, "The defendant can waive any right he wants as long as it was an informed decision and not coerced."

Bouchard remarked that if Judge Duffy upheld Klein's request, the arraignment in criminal court, which had just been postponed for a week, would not go forward. However, if the judge declined the defense attorney's request, the arraignment proceedings would continue.

At the hearing that day, Casey, Joe Fiorella, and Jacob Delashmutt appeared together in the courtroom once again.

This time they all sat together with a half-dozen television cameras aimed at them. Casey had his long straight hair pulled back in a neat ponytail. Delashmutt sported a vague goatee.

Shortly after the hearing was adjourned, Elyse Pahler's grandmother burst into tears while talking to a reporter who asked if she thought the boys should be executed for the murder.

"Of course, I'd like the death penalty. I'm a Christian, but I would still like the death penalty and so would my daughter."

Mrs. Walter, sixty-seven, then tapped a photo of her granddaughter she wore pinned to her heart.

"She was the love of my life."

Mrs. Walter told reporters she was already feeling frustrated by delays in the judicial process.

"I just want to see justice. What happened to Elyse could happen to anyone," she added.

But Elyse Walter was convinced that the alleged ritualistic nature of the killing was more common than most people thought.

"The public has got to wake up one of these days. It's not just their dogs and cats, but their children."

Mrs. Walter also echoed the prosecutor's charges by

recounting that the defendants had stalked the teenager and planned to kill her once before, but the attempt was aborted. Elyse's grandmother said that Elyse had told her parents that she thought the boys were stalking her, but they did not think anything about it. "You know kids," she said.

Mrs. Walter's comments were provoked because she had information about the slaying that hadn't been made public. However, she was reluctant to go into any detail even though she had seen court documents that spelled out the horrific details of Elyse's death at the hands of her assailants.

Meanwhile Elyse's father arrived late for that day's hearing, and missed the chance to see the boys accused of killing his daughter face-to-face. He pledged to make sure he saw them at their next court appearance.

Many of those involved with the case by this time were refusing to comment publicly about Elyse's killing because of the gag order.

An order sealing court records from scrutiny also prevented details of the case from becoming public.

But none of this stopped the Pahler family from continuing to show up at every court appearance made by the three suspects.

At the end of one hearing, newsmen crowded around Lisanne Pahler and asked her if it made her feel any better to see that her daughter's alleged killers had been caught and were now being dealt with.

"Absolutely not," she replied.

As Elyse's grandmother pointed out, "We will never be happy until we go to our graves."

Watching the faces of the boys accused of killing their beloved Elyse didn't make the pain and heartache any better, but it did at least allow them to try and come to terms with what had happened.

Twenty

There is no harder jail time than in a county lockup, especially for a teenager. Virtually no exercise, no stereo, a little television, few books, and even fewer visitors to break the monotony. Fiorella, Casey, and Delashmutt's days in the jail were interrupted only by occasional small chores.

Their lives were full of despair. By this time none of them were allowed to talk to each other in case they spoke about the murder and how it happened. Delashmutt and Fiorella remained outraged that Casey had told authorities what had happened.

Except for their families, an occasional friend, and the attorneys representing them, the boys had few visitors. They were locked up in the San Luis Obispo County Jail, alone and apprehensive.

None of the boys had any hope of being acquitted of the murder and released from custody. Casey had confessed to playing a role in what happened but denied committing the actual murder, and although Fiorella and Delashmutt had refused to talk to detectives, they had talked to enough other people prior to their arrest to make their conviction a near certainty, or so prosecutors and investigators hoped.

Except for the few days that they were given psychological evaluations at area hospitals, their hours were spent waiting for their next court appearance.

Their only hope was to be tried as juveniles instead of adults. If convicted as juveniles, they stood a chance of getting out of prison while still relatively young. If tried as adults, they would inevitably spend the rest of their lives in prison.

On September 16, 1996, Jacob Delashmutt, Royce Casey, and Joe Fiorella appeared in the Superior Court at San Luis Obispo, and each pleaded not guilty to murder and rape charges.

They all seemed resigned, emotionally unattached to what was happening around them or the task ahead. Their skin was the pale milky color that comes from months in prison. They had now been incarcerated for almost six months and had acquired the demeanor of people resigned to serving long sentences. They were all thinner, but a rigorous weight program at the county jail had given their arms and shoulders some definition.

Yet none of them were totally indifferent, as they appeared to the crowd. In fact, they looked a tad embarrassed. They glanced to the back of the courtroom, where several classmates sat.

Despite now being scheduled to be prosecuted as

adults, observers predicted that the sluggish judicial pace was unlikely to pick up because of the complex nature of the charges and age of the defendants.

Attorneys for each suspect indicated they were intending to continue challenging "special findings" alleged by prosecutors before any preliminary hearing could be held.

David Hurst, representing Fiorella, said prosecutors were improperly using those findings—such as the allegations that Elyse Pahler was tortured—to justify decisions about where the defendants should be imprisoned if convicted.

Superior Court Judge Christopher Money then postponed the preliminary hearing because one defense attorney had only recently been assigned to the case.

Delashmutt's lawyer, Theresa Klein, said she still intended to appeal within twenty days the juvenile court judge's ruling allowing her client to give up his right to a hearing in that court.

On October 2, 1996, Fiorella's attorney Dave Hurst asked the court to consider a motion to exclude the public from the upcoming preliminary hearing on the case. Hurst argued that pretrial publicity had already adversely influenced potential jurors and endangered his client's guarantee of a fair trial.

He told Judge Christopher Money that because the case had received both "regionwide and nationwide notoriety," further comment by the press and the parties involved would only add to the publicity surrounding the case and thereby endanger his client's guarantee of a fair trial.

However, Deputy District Attorney Dan Bouchard had his doubts that closing the hearing would be necessary to ensure that an adequate, unbiased jury pool could be assembled if the case did go to trial, as he assumed it would at that time.

"I am always amazed what people don't know about cases," Bouchard told reporters outside the courtroom afterward. "If it's not an immediate part of their lives, they may read about it and forget it."

When asked if the various motions and requests by defense counsels had slowed down the judicial process, Bouchard defended the legal maneuvering and court schedule. "The system has to accommodate reasonable needs of the defense to be prepared," he said.

Although the deputy district attorney acknowledged that the time taken to schedule the preliminary hearing had been unusually long, the prosecutor pointed out that Delashmutt had retained new attorneys, and they needed time to adequately review their client's case.

Barry Post and Jeffrey Scott Yanuk, from Sherman Oaks, near Los Angeles, then took over Delashmutt's defense from Theresa Klein, who had been the suspect's second attorney after Jeffrey Stein resigned from the case more than a month earlier. Stein had been privately retained while Post was recommended to Delashmutt's parents by another Southern California defense counsel.

Royce Casey had also switched attorneys earlier that same month. He was now represented by Barry Schiavo of San Luis Obispo, who replaced Kevin McReynolds.

It was becoming clear that the youths were far from settled about what they were going to concede in relation to their involvement in the death of Elyse Pahler.

* * *

On October 23, 1996, the last chapter was written in the case of the two teenagers accused of beating an Arroyo Grande woman with a baseball bat in her home.

The case was significant because it had come at a time when the entire city was feeling as if violent crimes committed by youths were rampant following the death of Elyse Pahler and the homicide allegedly committed by Joe Fiorella's best friend Travis Williams.

Joshua Garner, eighteen, pleaded guilty to prosecution charges of assault with a deadly weapon plus attempted robbery and two burglaries. He was sentenced to eight years and four months.

Matthew Schandel, accused of actually hitting the defenseless woman with the bat, was given twelve years and four months for attempted murder.

On Thursday, November 14, 1996, Superior Court Judge Christopher Money preserved the public's right to observe the legal proceedings leading up to the probable trial of the three suspects. Attorney David Hurst's request had been denied.

In making his decision to permit the public into the courtroom, Judge Money considered the standards of public access set down by the United States Supreme Court. In this case, he ruled that the public's right to observe legal proceedings outweighed the argument that pretrial publicity might prejudice potential jurors.

But Judge Money was not unsympathetic to Hurst's complaint and agreed to exclude all electronic recording devices and cameras from the preliminary hearings. He also reserved his right to clear the courtroom during testimony of the prosecutors' expert witnesses if that testimony was inappropriate for the public to hear. Court officials had indicated earlier that any hearing in which records of illicit drug use were referred would be closed to the public.

Defense attorney Hurst reminded the court in his motion that testimony at a preliminary hearing usually came only from the prosecution's side. It is then that prosecutors had to show the court that they had enough evidence to warrant taking the case to trial.

Attorneys for the defendants were not required to expose their strategy for defending their clients at that time. They could save that for the trial, when the jury and the prosecution would hear the evidence at the same time. For that reason, defense attorneys often remained silent during the preliminary hearings except to ask questions to clarify information offered by the district attorney's office.

Lawyers representing the local media said they were satisfied with the judge's decision. One attorney commented, "It was a very thoughtful decision, one in which he applied the standards of the United States Supreme Court and fortunately came down on the side of public access."

But it was noted by all present that Judge Money could still again raise the issue of not allowing television and film cameras into the courtroom if he so desired. The judge said he made his decision "without prejudice," meaning that he would entertain future motions presumably from the representatives of the television media to open the hearings to their cameras.

On that same day, Judge Money also ruled that the two youngest defendants—Fiorella and Delashmutt—would not face special findings in the case against them.

Money insisted that prosecutors could not charge the teenagers with allegations of torture, rape, mayhem, and exceptional depravity.

His decision echoed an earlier ruling in June, 1996, by juvenile court Judge Michael Duffy. The issue hinged on the fact that the law did not specify murder defendants between fourteen and sixteen years old being eligible for a life sentence without possibility of parole if convicted.

Deputy District Attorney Dodie Harman said after the decision that even though Judge Money ruled the jury would not hear the special circumstances, she could still ask the judge to consider those findings in rendering sentence at the end of the trial.

Although the ruling gave an unexpected boost to defendants Fiorella and Delashmutt and their families, Harman said the decision would have little or no impact on the prosecution's presentation of their case. The prosecutors could still have a jury hear evidence of the acts alleged in the special circumstances.

Ironically, it was now Casey—who went to authorities and volunteered to lead sheriff's investigators to the crime scene and Elyse's body—who faced the possibility of the stiffer sentence of life without the possibility of parole.

In that same courtroom just a few weeks later, another judge ruled that Joe Fiorella's best friend Travis Williams should face a separate trial from his accomplice on the murder and burglary charges stemming from their alleged killing spree at the house of an elderly Arroyo Grande woman.

Williams, seventeen, and his codefendant Tommy Traughber, eighteen, of Grover City, were each ordered to attend separate trials in the spring of 1997.

It was disclosed that the prosecution intended to use statements from each of the teenage defendants in which they pointed fingers at each other over who actually killed the old lady.

In Arroyo Grande many residents were still bewildered by the spate of violent crimes committed by schoolchildren from their city.

"It was as if a peaceful little backwater had exploded into murder and mayhem," said one resident. "It was all so sudden that some of us started to wonder if there was something in the water that had affected these children.

"But one thing was for sure: Arroyo Grande would never be the same again."

Twenty-one

Shannon Plotner and Angel Katyryni sat alone at the counter of the Burger King in the center of Arroyo Grande, quietly munching on doughnuts as the regulars wandered in for their morning coffee.

Life in the town was never quite the same again after Elyse Pahler's death. Her best friends Angel and Shannon didn't mix much with other students.

In the yard at the Arroyo Grande High School, they would more often than not talk just between themselves during breaks between classes.

The girls had developed a suspicious nature and mistrust of people since Elyse's disappearance.

"We just felt kinda strange, as if we couldn't trust anyone," Shannon later explained.

Angel often slept over at Shannon's house in the middle of Arroyo Grande, and the two girls would find themselves aimlessly wandering the streets of the town.

They were bored but reluctant to go to the same places they visited with Elyse because of the painful memories.

"I kept remembering how we all hung out together. During that last month before she disappeared, we would take the bus to town and walk everywhere together," said Shannon.

Often those memories of their good friend would reduce them to tears, and they'd have to retreat back to Shannon's mother's duplex just around the corner from the town's only movie theater—where all three girls had watched *Interview With the Vampire* so many times.

"Sometimes I think back to those days when Elyse was alive, and I realize she gave us so much," says Angel. "Elyse was such fun to be around that she made our lives so much more enjoyable."

At least the photo album that Elyse's mother Lisanne gave to the girls, following the arrest of the three suspects, did remind them of the good times. Shannon and Angel would often stay at home and just sit and look through the pictures over and over again.

"We liked remembering all those good things about Elyse, and the photos kind of make her come back to life," explained Shannon.

Shannon also kept a copy of the missing poster that was issued by the police and her family just a few days after she disappeared. "It reminds me of what happened," she says. "But it's such a great picture of Elyse. So typical of her."

Neither of the girls ever went to the court to see the three suspects accused of murdering their best friend. But in a place as small as Arroyo Grande, they inevitably encountered friends of the boys.

"We tried to ignore them. It's kinda strange because

so many kids knew more about what had happened to Elyse than they admitted at the time,'' explained Shannon.

The two girls were also continually haunted by the thought that they did not do enough to help police find Elyse earlier.

''There were so many clues—and most of them could have been found at the high school,'' added Angel: ''Everyone knew that Jacob and Joe were into some kind of satanism. And we also knew all about their death metal band. There were so many rumors about them. But everyone just looked on them as creeps not worth talking to.

''We had so many ideas on where Elyse had gone, but we thought she'd be back. How wrong could we be? Many of the clues were just staring us in the face. Why didn't we work it out? Why?''

Despite those close shaves with the boys following Elyse's death, neither Shannon nor Angel say they are afraid of the suspects.

''They're just crazy, mixed-up kids. Sure, they were creepy, but we never felt scared of them. Sometimes I wish we had been more freaked by them because then we might have done something or told someone about them.

''It's weird because we felt they were watching us all the time, trying to find out what we knew. But we never worked out why. How could we have been so dumb?''

Shannon says she'll never forget that day at the campsite when Joe Fiorella was watching her as the four boys tried to persuade her to go for a walk with them.

''Joe never talked. He said nothing. But his eyes were on me the whole time. Jacob and Royce did all the talking. I hate to think about what they might have done to me."

Both girls are now on good terms with the Pahlers, although they have hardly seen the family since they moved to San Luis Obispo shortly after Elyse's disappearance.

"That's the only good part about them finding Elyse. It made the family realize we had nothing to do with what happened to her," Angel explained.

"Yeah, it kinda freaked me to feel—like we did— that they thought we were hiding something from them," Shannon added. "But then, none of this will bring back Elyse, and that's all that matters."

Angel and Shannon still say that the worst thing about the aftermath is that children at Arroyo Grande High School continue to make tasteless jokes about what happened to their best friend.

"It's made me realize just how sick many of these kids are. They seem to get a kick outta saying that her body was mutilated, that some of her limbs were hacked off."

Other children even brag to this day about knowing the defendants.

Says Shannon, "They say they know them just to act macho. It's so pathetic, and I don't understand it. These guys took our friend away from us. They don't deserve any admiration."

Both Shannon and Angel acknowledge that the tedium of life in such a quiet place as Arroyo Grande may have contributed to the death of Elyse.

"There's nothing to do around here. It's so boring. That's why kids get wrapped up in music like death metal. What else are they supposed to do?"

Both girls also concede that the sort of television and movies consumed by kids may have had an influence.

"I think too many of these kids watch really gruesome horror movies and think that killing people is kinda cool. Why don't their parents do something to make them realize death is bad?"

Angel and Shannon have carefully avoided the so-called Pipe of Death since well before Elyse disappeared, and they say that few of the kids on the mesa will go near the place now.

"It's kinda associated with those boys. Nobody wants to hang out there anymore," says Angel.

"Before Elyse was found lots of kids would go out there, smoke crank, drink, and play around. But now everyone's a bit scared because they realize that Elyse was lying there so close by for so long."

Both girls remain puzzled as to why the police made so little effort to find Elyse after she first disappeared.

"Obviously, they just thought that Elyse had run away with some guy or something," said Shannon.

Angel still remembers exactly how she told investigators she thought Elyse had met with Delashmutt, Fiorella, and Casey the day of her disappearance. She also told them how the boys had knocked Elyse down that bank near her home.

"But they did nothing. I don't even know if they went to interview the boys. But obviously they didn't find out anything," says Angel.

The girls are reluctant to completely blame the police, but they do feel that there are still many unanswered questions about Elyse's death.

Says Shannon, "What happened to Elyse kinda showed up Arroyo Grande to be the sort of place where no one wants to know about what's really going on. It's easier just to sweep it all under the carpet and forget about it.

"Well, this time there's no way anyone can forget what happened to Elyse."

Reporters like Tom Parsons of the *Five Cities Times Press Recorder* were assigned the task of following the complicated legal arguments that precluded the full criminal trials of Delashmutt, Fiorella, and Casey.

"They have been projecting the summer as the eventual date of the trials, but it's difficult to know when they will get through the preliminary level first," explained Parsons in February, 1997.

He believed that all three defendants would eventually plea to lesser charges and the full, horrifying story of what really happened that night in July, 1995, would never actually be fully revealed.

"The sordid details will not come out if they plead guilty, and that must be the way the family would like it," added Parsons.

The veteran reporter recalled that the Pahlers have been trying to protect the good name of their daughter ever since her body was discovered in March, 1996.

Parsons says he is well aware there are many more gruesome details about the circumstances surrounding Elyse Pahler's death, which have so far only been touched upon.

"She actually left the house that night because she wanted some dope. They promised her some kind of narcotics. When they gave it to her, it wasn't what she

expected and her resistance was lowered," claimed Parsons.

In February, 1997, Elyse Neilson Walter voiced the family's frustrations with the drawn-out legal process that
was preventing Delashmutt, Casey, and Fiorella from
coming to trial as quickly as possible.

Walter was particularly anxious that the trials should
get under way because each time the youths appeared in
court, there was a flurry of publicity that dragged everything up yet again.

"It's so difficult for David and Lisanne. They'll never
recover from the loss of Elyse, but the nightmare keeps
being compounded by the publicity the case attracts
every time it comes to court.

"It's got so bad that now we just wait from one day
to the next to see what's going to happen."

Many of those close to the case believed that all three
boys would eventually plead guilty to lesser charges in
order to prevent the full, gruesome story of Elyse's death
being broadcast across the nation.

"If they continue denying the charges, the eventual
trials will last at least several months each, and I think
they realize that it would be more humane to spare
everyone involved such an ordeal," added the attorney.

The other problem facing the judicial process in San
Luis Obispo County was that there had been such an
increase in crime over the previous eighteen months that
the judge assigned the Elyse Pahler case had two other
murder trials to deal with ahead of that case.

"Not long ago the police in this county were com-
plaining that they never had any real crimes to deal with

up here. But suddenly there has been a dramatic increase in crime, and most of it is juvenile,'' explained the local attorney.

A lengthy sexual harassment trial against a local prison also threatened to logjam the judicial process even further. ''This is creating a feeling of complete uncertainty as to when the trials will really happen.''

Meanwhile it was believed the gag order—called a protective order—would remain in force until a jury had been selected if the boys continued to deny the charges.

''The ultimate point is to give yourself a fair and impartial jury,'' added the lawyer. ''Without this any trial would be a complete farce, and we have to avoid this at all costs.''

Twenty-two

A crucial part of the three suspects' defense strategy would be an extensive evaluation of their medical condition at the time they were alleged to have killed Elyse Pahler. Forensic psychiatrists and child psychologists carried out numerous interviews with them at the San Luis Obispo County Jail.

These "mind experts" are called into every major homicide case soon after the arrest of a suspect. Their modus operandi is to initially interview the subjects having deliberately done the minimum of research on the case. Often nothing more than a newspaper clipping is read in advance of that first meeting, because the mind experts prefer to hear a full account of a suspect's alleged crime in his or her words with their own interpretation of exactly what happened. That alone helps the psychiatrist or psychologist during initial evaluation of a crime.

After that first interview is concluded, the mind experts begin a painstaking research process that includes collecting information from a vast range of sources, including relatives, medical notes, school reports, comments from employers, and witness statements for both defense and prosecution. Notes that police have collected about a subject's background can also often prove useful.

If the defendants have got a psychiatric history then notes and even GP's comments are obtained. Then there follows a series of much more intense interviews with the subjects.

It is vital here to outline the major differences between forensic psychologists and psychiatrists, because there tends to be a good deal of overlap between the two professions. The psychologist is not usually medically qualified, having studied pure psychology and the development of the mind. The clinical psychologist judges a subject based on his or her abnormalities and is trained to carry out a certain range of checks that require a practicing certificate. Part of that investigative process is in forensic work. However, a forensic psychiatrist is not qualified to give those same tests. They require a specific form of training and usually come from a general medical background, then go on to specialize in psychiatry. They alone are empowered to prescribe people with drugs.

The most important single factor when it comes to the role of a psychiatrist or psychologist is to evaluate whether someone is different from the average man in the street. What changed them? And are they capable of doing it again?

Forensic psychiatrist Dr. Peter Wood is one of the

world's foremost experts in what drives people to kill, having worked on more than 400 death-related cases over the past fifteen years. He says: "There isn't a correlation between severity of offenses and mental problems. You can be very normal and kill someone. Naturally, I have a familiarity with the territory, but one must never get away from the shock horror of somebody who has killed someone else. To detach from the emotion that people feel about homicide is quite natural in my profession. But, by the same token, it is very important not to get out of step with the way people in general feel about murder. Otherwise you become too blasé about it."

Even after that first interview with a defendant, the mind expert will rough out a report on a suspect. They will have gone to great lengths to ensure that the subject interviewed did not get distressed. After all, that first meeting is a starting point for what will eventually be formally written up for the actual trial. The mind expert sets up a series of questions for the defendant. A lot of the time it is remarkably easy to tell if someone is of normal intelligence or not.

Often there are clear indications. The difficult cases are the ones where the subjects have done something inexplicable, and they themselves seem totally ordinary. Certainly there are elements of this in the case outlined in this book despite the problems that existed in the background of certain family members of the defendants.

The key questions that will be asked at the eventual trial of all three youths will be: What was in their minds when the alleged crimes were committed? What motivated the offenses? The experts will want to re-create every step taken by the defendants in an effort to repeat the events exactly as they occurred, so that a full picture of the killing can be properly revealed. Experts now believe such careful analysis not only assists ongoing trials, but can help avoid future tragedies.

Criminal psychiatrists are convinced some groups of people will almost definitely re-offend. These are the ones where great care and attention must be paid when considering an application for an early release from a custodial sentence.

The system for careful mental analysis of defendants has become an integral part of the justice system over the past twenty years. As a result, the cases of repeat homicides are decreasing. The one exception to the rule is that there are still a lot of people who kill children, are then imprisoned, only to get released and commit similar offenses again.

Undoubtedly, where the victim is a child, there is a greater risk of repetition. The average sentence served for child homicide or manslaughter in many so-called civilized countries like the United States is less than ten years. Usually it is men in their late teens or early twenties who commit many of these offenses. By the time they are in their early thirties, many of them have served a sentence, got out again, and are at an age when, by definition, they are going to be in a position to kill again.

There has also been a disturbing increase in the number of teenagers who become involved in murder in similar circumstances as is described here.

One of forensic expert Dr. Peter Wood's most recent cases featured a female baby-sitter, aged just eleven, who killed a child in her care. The case left Wood with a clear impression of what drives children—especially teenagers—to kill.

"There are usually serious things wrong in their own childhood," explained Dr. Wood. "They failed to learn how to limit their behavior because of their own experiences. A child often has to become totally amoral in order to survive. If you have to fight your way through childhood because you are being mistreated, you don't grow up with the right limitations on your own behavior."

Sometimes the defendant will even try to put a romantic glow on their childhood, when, in fact, they had a very miserable time.

"A lot of people will say, 'Well, my father used to belt me, but I deserved it,' " explained Dr. Wood. "Then I would say, 'What did you have to do to get belted,' and they would say, 'If I was home late from school and had dirty knees.' I would say, 'Isn't that a little excessive' and they would say, 'Maybe.' "

One of the biggest problems facing Delashmutt, Casey, and Fiorella—besides the obvious seriousness of the charges they are facing—is the public outcry that followed their arrest in March, 1996. That response of shock and horror that three youths could allegedly cut down one of their peers is a very human reaction, but it sparked fears that any potential jurors would be tainted by the constant flow of publicity that has accompanied the case.

As one senior attorney involved in the case explained: "When people are accused of such heinous crimes, there is a real danger that the public will judge them guilty before a trial has taken place."

In the San Luis Obispo County Jail, the youths continued to be kept in almost permanent solitary confinement because of concerns over their safety from inside and outside those prison walls.

However, many mind experts like Dr. Peter Wood often look on the accused as the "victims." Something inside their family life and background can provoke the ultimate act of revenge. It will be interesting to see how defending attorneys handle such aspects in the coming trials of the three suspects.

Psychologists also say that undoubtedly the guilt—even if it is not apparent in many defendants—will continue to haunt the accused for the rest of their lives.

Dr. Wood added: "Most of them are haunted, broken, victims of the crimes they have committed, from which there is no escape."

The biggest single common denominator among some of the most notorious killers in recent years has been their extraordinary ability to create a so-called mask of sanity.

In other words, the accused's dark and sinister behavior is often masked by a veneer of very good and socially rewarding activities. This mask has, according to experts like Dr. Joel Norris—PhD in psychology and a founding member of the International Committee of Neuroscientists to Study Episodic Aggression—manifested itself through grandiosity or a belief in one's own superhuman importance, hypervigilance, or an extraordinary concern about acting morally and properly, and social adeptness to the point of extreme manipulative ability.

Many defendants often demonstrate the basic attributes of an effective manager (or parent). "The ability to get other people to do what you want them to do," ex-

plained Dr. Norris. Many are strangely capable of sensing the inferiority in others, the need to be dominated
and told what to do, and the desperate need for approval.
Those under the spell of such people tend to appear on
the outside to be normal, upstanding males and/or females, albeit with free spirits. But actually, they are
more often than not deeply scarred people who actively
seek domination as a missing component in their own
personalities.

By possessing that keen sense of what is required to
conform to the outward trappings of society, people who
kill others are often able to exhibit acceptable—indeed,
exemplary—behavior in their own communities. "Their
need for approval and their ability to second-guess con-
frontation is so great that they go undetected by the public at large," adds Dr. Norris.

The qualities that compel people to murder are eerily
similar to those qualities that American society expects
from successful individuals. They often see themselves
as "doing good," having penetrated the very society
they hated so much.

But there is one part of the personality of a killer that
remains in all of us—the need to be accepted and the
will to achieve. In the case of the accused youths, there
can be no actual satisfying or satiating it, whereas normally developed people can decide when to be "selfish"
and preserve quality time for themselves. Dr. Norris and
other experts say that virtually all such killers have little
or no self-esteem—psychobiologically, many of them
cannot determine the boundaries of their own selves and
thus cannot conceive of themselves as having separate
identities—and this is the factor that so contributes to
their eventual explosion of violence.

This means that most of them have spent a lifetime repressing the cancerous rage at the core of their personalities. A progressive and escalating loss of control and sense of madness becomes apparent to them from the time they first become aware of their own dark, primal urges. Such people learn to hate and fear their own evil side yet cannot help but succumb to them in moments of pure reactive violence. However, they often develop a chameleonlike mask of sanity or normalcy whose purpose is to protect them from the turbulent and hostile violent central element of their psyches. This mask of sanity also camouflages them from the society they have learned to fear and hate.

During this period in an episodic killer's development, a unique set of mechanisms emerges, composed of the same elements that make for sociopathy or sociopathic and multiple personalities, and these interact with the neurological impairments that cause significant but convenient losses of memory and gaps in reality: the episodes during which the series of killings are committed. "The drive to live within society, the ability to hope and dream about the possibilities the future holds for them, and the sense of self that allows them to benefit from personal and vocational achievements have all been physically or emotionally beaten away from them in their earlier years," explained Dr. Norris, providing an eerie insight into the life of murderers.

Another characteristic of such episodic killers is that they become pathological liars. On the one hand, lying is simply an extension of that chameleonlike ability to blend in with their background. They sense the information that people around them want to hear and provide it. "Truth is not an issue for them," says Dr. Norris. "Survival is."

Truth also demands that a person perceive a modicum of self-worth. Most episodically violent individuals see themselves as having no real worth and no meaning for life; they are honest neither with themselves nor with others. On a practical level, say the experts, lying is a form of manipulation. If one can lie successfully, one can get others to believe what one wants them to. But when lying becomes chronic in the schoolchild or in the person whose recapitulation of basic facts may change from day to day, it is a clear indicator of other serious behavioral disorders. Dr. Norris believes that most episodic killers sincerely believe the stories they are telling when they are telling them.

Twenty-three

So-called mind experts have already delved into the family history of all the defendants from well before they ever met Elyse Pahler. They have probed the youths' entire childhoods for evidence of incidents that might help to explain their later actions. All their parents' attitudes toward crucial elements of the boys' upbringing like sex, money, and love will also have shaped their later social problems. Undoubtedly, the breakup of Joe Fiorella's parents' marriage will be considered as a significant turning point in his childhood.

In some other recent killing cases, the death of a parent or grandparent has been cited by mind experts as a possible cause of resentment that gradually built up into a crescendo of horrific violence. Psychologists insist that many killers have an obsession with death that is fueled by earlier experiences, be it through real life, movies, or music.

Only in the past few years have professionals begun to understand the process through which such ultimately malevolent individuals have been created in each generation. These experts are now coming to appreciate how such episodic violence is shaped by patterns of child abuse, pathologically negative parenting, brain injuries resulting from physical traumas, inherited neurological disorders, chronic malnutrition, chronic drug and alcohol abuse, and even toxic poisoning from environmental pollutants.

There is a very common cycle of deprivation that involves the repetition of often similar offenses a generation later or sometimes even two generations later. Public health officials even concede that such cycles of violence in all their various forms have been spawned from previous generations. "Parents who abuse their children, physically as well as psychologically, install in them an almost instinctive reliance upon violence as a first resort to any challenge," says Dr. Joel Norris. "Each generation teaches the next generation to react with violence, often reinforced and compounded by the media. Those patterns of violent behavior spread, consuming increasingly greater numbers of victims."

Dr. Norris is particularly critical of the way that, until recently, many killers tended to be treated as either sociopaths or psychopaths and were immediately relegated to the care of the criminal justice system. "They are treated as though they were within the range of normal human existence, yet had willingly become deviant," explained Dr. Norris. "But this is not the case. They are non-personality types who eventually come alive only during the act of murder. However, because the criminal justice system concentrates on apprehension and punishment, rather than on discovering the causality of violence and preventing its spread, individuals who display this type of medical syndrome have slid through the system untreated.''

Dr. Norris believes that this lack of understanding has directly helped increase the number of killers in our midsts. ''The infection has been allowed to spread through society like a plague: the emerging killers are the carriers, transmitting the syndrome from one generation to the next.''

The murder of Elyse Pahler presents an extraordinary opportunity for criminal experts to examine in minute detail the background and circumstances of a killing that is unique in its very nature because of the young age of the victim and her alleged killers.

In the eyes of many, Joe Fiorella, Jacob Delashmutt, and Royce Casey should qualify as first-degree murderers if found guilty of the charges they face in relationship to the death of Elyse Pahler.

Criminologists across the globe will be watching this case closely. As acknowledged expert on murder Marvin Wolfgang said: ''Homicide can be 'caused' by practically any type of major psychiatric illness.''

Other forensic psychiatrists are particularly intrigued by the case: ''It is extraordinary in itself that they allegedly stalked and killed this young girl in the manner that has been alleged. But to then involve acts of satanism and devil worship is even more unusual.''

The most significant allegation concerning the supposed crimes of Delashmutt, Casey, and Fiorella is that prosecutors believe Elyse Pahler was deliberately

tracked down because she was a virgin whom they
wanted to sacrifice.

"They are less likely to be psychotic because they
involved others. If you are driven by delusion, unless
you draw someone else into your own delusions, the
motive for killing is foreign to the person you are trying
to involve in your behavior. Almost by definition, people
who kill jointly are not psychotic. That's the simplest
way of putting it," explained one expert.

One of the most astonishing aspects of the case—
whatever the outcome—is that it took police so long to
even establish that Elyse Pahler had been brutally murdered rather than a runaway as they had believed for
nine months. Defendant Royce Casey's efforts in alert-
ing authorities to the killing have already been well documented in this book, but there is another aspect that
has so far been overlooked—the apparent unwillingness
of police to even suspect she might have been killed
after disappearing from her home that July evening, even
though it was clear that she was both a loving daughter
and an enthusiastic high school student.

Many criminologists believe that too much emphasis
is being put on profiling killers. Often, some insist, these
profiles prove wholly—or certainly partially—inaccurate. In the case of Elyse's initial disappearance, investigators believed they did not have enough clues to even
launch a murder hunt.

Privately, police in San Luis Obispo County say that
was the precise reason why so little action was taken
initially to locate missing Elyse.

Yet in the past decade police homicide units have become far more sophisticated in their investigations and
tracking of killers. Detectives tended to be strictly re-

active up until ten years ago. When a murder was reported, investigators gathered what evidence they could, traced the victim's identity, and tried to reconstruct the crime from what they could determine about the victim's movements during his or her final hours. If there were witnesses, they were interviewed also. But this procedure fails miserably when dealing with apparently motiveless killings. The reason for this is simple: Such crimes do not fit into any set pattern. The motive for murder is not dependent upon the particular situation or upon the individual victim (without a body or any clues as to the alleged nature of the Elyse's death, police were left with next to nothing).

The truth of the matter is that reactive homicide investigations depend upon things like: weight of evidence, clues at the crime scene, relationship between the victim and the murderer, involved witnesses or passersby, and, finally, the fear and guilt of the killer. In the case of Elyse, the police were virtually empty-handed until Royce Casey decided to tell them what he claimed had happened.

The alleged killers of Elyse Pahler were never even the target of a combined task force until after her body was discovered, and that finally persuaded investigators to act upon Casey's claims.

Following the uncovering of the body, detectives only had a crime scene as evidence. They had absolutely nothing else to go on until after the autopsy, and even that medical examination did not really provide many additional clues other than incidentals. They also faced further investigatorial problems because Elyse had died eight months earlier in an open-air location where the forces of nature were constantly at work. This created, in effect, two crime scenes and made the detectives' job much harder until they began a piece-by-piece search into the backgrounds of the boys and their victim. But again, this was *after* Casey's story had finally been believed. Interestingly, many experts believe that the killer (or killers) who kills in a remote location is definitely more in control.

Another factor that undoubtedly helped the alleged killers of Elyse Pahler avoid detection for so long was the lack of publicity Elyse's disappearance attracted. Page two news in local newspapers was hardly enough to raise any real interest outside of Arroyo Grande. In retrospect, the lack of any real press and TV coverage for Elyse's disappearance helped dampen the police efforts.

If the case had received more publicity, then someone further afield might have recognized the description of the missing girl and done something about it. (Although it has to be pointed out that Elyse was only outside her home for a matter of minutes before being taken to the eucalyptus grove).

Detectives have also speculated that at least two of Elyse's alleged killers found it easy to put the murder into the back of their minds, because there were so few reminders of their crime in the newspaper and on the television.

What is important about the profile of a killer from a policeman's point of view is that it is impossible to see a complete picture of the criminal's motivation until well after he or she has been apprehended and diagnosed. Current police training still focuses on the traditional murderer who is not compelled to murder and who flees because he fears the police and prosecution.

Meanwhile the episodic killer will go on committing enough crimes to ensure his own destruction. What made the alleged killers of Elyse Pahler so difficult to apprehend was that they apparently stopped killing.

One senior homicide detective summed it up by saying: "The breaks usually only come by chance." Another crucial aspect of the initial police investigation was whether the killer or killers were confident enough to spend time at the crime scene or whether they felt the need to leave it immediately after the killing, since no one found the body of Elyse until detectives were led to it.

From some incidents recalled by relatives and school friends, the teenagers appeared paranoid. It is conceivable that the alleged killers of Elyse Pahler were suffering from delusions at the time that the blond teenager was murdered.

These alleged killers seem to have been completely wrapped up in their own feelings and obsessions. Their self-imposed seclusion from many of their classmates appears to be clear evidence of their introverted state at the time.

Doctors will spend many months gently coaxing these alleged killers to confess their true motives for ending the life of another teenager. It may well be that the forensic experts queuing up to interview Delashmutt, Casey, and Fiorella will find problems in extracting information about their true feelings. Their life in Arroyo Grande following the death of Elyse Pahler clearly indicates that they had neatly compartmentalized the killings so that they only thought about it when they wanted.

But there are strong indications that the boys had become completely paranoid about Elyse's friends at school. They felt that pupils were constantly spying on them, running them down, and speculating whether they were actually involved in the disappearance of Elyse.

Researchers typically examine the family life of defendants to try and uncover the motivations behind the crime they allegedly committed.

Most violence in the family is perpetrated by parents against their children. Researchers have established that there are three basic categories of violence against children.

1. Ordinary violence, hitting and slapping, is by far the largest category—approximately 97 percent of all children are struck at least once a year.

2. Severe violence is prevalent in almost nine million youngsters in the United States between the ages of three and seventeen. They are victims of "assaultive acts that go beyond pushing, slapping, and throwing things and which therefore carry a high risk of causing injury serious enough to require medical attention, i.e., kicking, punching, beating up, stabbing, and shooting."

3. Then there is very serious violence when lasting injury and sometimes even death is inflicted.

Yet, despite all the facts and figures and horror stories, society persists in its idealization of the family as an island of peace in a savage, chaotic world. Incidents of family violence are drastically underreported, while accounts of violence perpetrated by strangers continue to find their way into banner headlines.

Though society's refusal to acknowledge and begin to

deal with the gruesome reality of family violence seems perplexing on the surface, it is not difficult given the family's sacrosanct importance to society. No one doubts that the exercise of strong parental authority, especially in a child's formative years, is essential to healthy, normal development. Consequently, however, parents wield an unparalleled degree of influence and power over their children, who are completely dependent upon them.

It has only been in recent history that society has openly admitted that some parents abuse that sacred power entrusted to them. It wasn't until 1984 that the federal government formally recognized family violence as a critical social problem by creating the Attorney General's Task Force on Family Violence. Notwithstanding these strides in recognition and changes in policy, the parental prerogative remains protected in many ways, a distinct double standard for judging victims and perpetrators of child abuse that still exists throughout society today. Paul Mones, a respected lawyer who specializes in defending children who kill, explained: "This double standard is evident in our social attitudes and in the legal system."

In the case of Elyse Pahler's murder, there was undoubtedly a very slow and gradual buildup to the killing. There is also a definite suggestion that it was a very calculated process.

It is highly likely that in the case of Delashmutt, Casey, and Fiorella a number of associates colluded in their alleged crime. "They did not blow the whistle on the killers," explained one expert, "even though they knew there were allegedly three killers in their midst."

The pressure that must have put some teenagers under would be unquestionable.

Many experts believe that killers in such circumstances like to pull in certain individuals and confide in them just to help ease their conscience. Also, they are emotionally immature and unable to cope with facing the full extent of their crimes alone.

Talking to a psychiatrist can often be far less traumatic than talking to the police, and it is entirely possible that the three suspects will reveal more about their alleged crimes and background through such meetings. The mind experts tend to cover the same ground as the official investigators, but in a different way.

Whatever happens to Jacob Delashmutt, Royce Casey, and Joe Fiorella, tragically there seems little doubt that the system will not follow through with extensive medical help after their trials in the summer of 1997. Often it is left to the discretion (and kindness) of a psychiatrist or psychologist to provide free help because defendants such as the three youths cannot afford the high cost of medical treatment. Most mind experts believe that subjects like Delashmutt, Casey, and Fiorella should continue seeing them for at least *ten years* after a conviction or acquittal. It remains to be seen what, if anything, can be done to help answer the dozens of so-far unanswered questions surrounding virtually every aspect of this astonishing case.

Twenty-four

On Wednesday, February 5, 1997, Joseph Fiorella pleaded "no contest" to murdering Elyse during a dramatic court appearance in San Luis Obispo. Perhaps not surprisingly, the Pahlers were disappointed that the youth did not after all have to go through a full trial.

After Fiorella's plea, Superior Court Judge Christopher G. Money asked the sixteen-year-old if he had stabbed Elyse to death.

"Yes, Your Honor," replied Fiorella somberly after briefly conferring with his attorney, David T. Hurst.

It later emerged that in exchange for the plea of murder, charges of stalking, rape, and torture had been dismissed, along with satanic implications, following a recommendation from Deputy District Attorney Dodie Harman.

There was also the matter of alleged sexual relations with Elyse's corpse, which was expected to be used by prosecutors to ensure the other two defendants face maximum sentences.

Initially, it had been expected that Delashmutt and Casey would also plead guilty to lesser charges, but by the middle of 1997 it was becoming clear that prosecutors did not intend to let them off the hook.

"The DA is not offering them a deal. It's as simple as that," insisted one court official.

If a full trial did go ahead for both boys, then much of the previously secret evidence that outlines in graphic detail what happened to Elyse the night she died will be publicly disclosed for the first time.

As one prominent member of the Arroyo Grande community pointed out, "It's going to be awful. They're going to drag it all up again, and this time they'll be all the details about her death that will be so painful for her family and friends."

The surprise decision to deal with Fiorella went ahead at short notice after Judge Money had ruled against applying special circumstances to Fiorella because he had been under sixteen years old at the time of the crime. The law had no provision for a more severe sentence than twenty-six years to life for defendants fifteen years of age and younger.

It was made clear that Fiorella would have to serve 85 percent of his sentence before he would be eligible for parole. But it was clear that his plea had major implications for the two remaining defendants in the case, Delashmutt and Casey.

Although Delashmutt was also only fifteen years old when Elyse Pahler was killed, there continued to be no indication that he would be offered the same plea deal as Fiorella.

Casey was still expected to face stiffer sentencing if and when he was actually convicted of taking part in the crime. It could well be a life sentence without parole even though it had been Casey who first brought the killing to the attention of police.

Prosecutors refused to say whether Fiorella would be recalled as a possible witness against his two alleged accomplices.

However, Fiorella's guilty plea meant that revealing probation reports could be publicly disclosed for the first time.

They consisted of interviews given by Fiorella in the days following his appearance in court for Elyse Pahler's murder. In the reports, Fiorella insisted that the school-girl's slaying had nothing to do with a satanic ritual and said there was never any talk of eating her body parts.

"I don't know where that came from," Fiorella told one youth probation officer.

In the report, the youth admitted that he would stay up night after night with friends listening to death metal groups like Slayer while using methamphetamine. It was "really affecting me," he said.

"It gets inside your head," said Fiorella, explaining the way he felt about the so-called death metal music. "It's almost embarrassing that I was so influenced by the music. It started to influence the way I looked at things."

Eric D. Shultz, the deputy probation officer who wrote the report on Fiorella, spoke twice at length to the youth.

The first interview was apparently brief, with Fiorella

commenting on his sentence, "It's a lot of time, but I guess it's appropriate."

But during his second interview, he was much more forthcoming and even expressed some remorse for the slaying.

"I wish it never happened. Since it's happened, I always wish that God can bring her back to life. I can imagine how her family must feel."

Fiorella even claimed he never had any intention of hurting anyone. "It was a stupid mistake."

Throughout the interview, Fiorella tried to minimize his own involvement in the girl's brutal killing, although he did confirm Casey's original version of events that Fiorella was the first to stab Elyse Pahler.

Fiorella said he stabbed the schoolgirl once or twice in the neck with a hunting knife, but insisted he did not plunge the six-inch blade all the way "because I couldn't stand the feel of the blade going into her neck."

But Fiorella contradicted Casey's story on other points. He claimed it was Casey who wanted to rape Pahler after she was stabbed and that he (Fiorella) had said, "Let's get out of here."

Fiorella said that Casey was the only source of the satanism links to Elyse's killing and even claimed that he did not know him well.

"I never hung out with Royce," said Fiorella to his probation officer. "Jacob got him involved."

Fiorella's claims are strongly disputed by the two other youths and Elyse's friends like Shannon Plotner and Angel Katyryni, who insist the three boys did hang out togther regularly.

However, Fiorella did admit throwing the murder

weapon into a nearby swamp he called "the pit of death" following the gruesome killing.

The youth openly confessed to using drugs, including methamphetamine "off and on," taking LSD "every other day," and smoking marijuana every day.

"I basically use with friends. It might sound like a lot to someone who doesn't use, but it's not that much."

At a preliminary hearing held on Wednesday, February 19, 1997, the two remaining defendants, Casey and Delashmutt, heard the district attorney's chief investigator Doug Odom tell the court in San Luis Obispo that Elyse Pahler's murder had been planned for "about a month and a half to two months" before it happened.

Both youths still faced six other felony counts—besides the murder—ranging from conspiracy to commit murder as members of a street gang, to torture, rape, and mayhem. They denied all the charges, although it was pointed out by prosecutors that both Delashmutt and Casey could plead guilty to first-degree murder and have all the other charges dismissed.

In exchange, they would receive the twenty-six years to life that Fiorella got at his sentencing following his plea bargain deal. (Ironically, neither of the youths would be likely to get stiffer sentences even if they went on trial and were convicted on all counts.)

Casey's lawyer, Barry Schiavo, later pointed out that such an agreement completely failed to acknowledge that it was his client who came forward and confessed to investigators eight months after Elyse's murder.

"I don't think that takes into account that he solved

the crime for them,'' Schiavo told reporters following the hearing.

The court heard how Casey had been trying to distance himself from Delashmutt and Fiorella ever since the killing and his genuine fear that they were planning to murder him.

The chief investigator for the district attorney, Doug Odom, testified that Casey told him the other two were planning another sacrifice of a young girl following Elyse's murder. It was also said that Delashmutt and Fiorella had openly described themselves as ''Satan's children'' and that the sacrifice was necessary to receive power from the devil so they could play the guitar better in their death metal band, Hatred.

As graphic details of the night of Elyse's death were disclosed by Odom, the courtroom fell into an eerie silence. Elyse's parents and grandparents listened and looked on without moving, almost hypnotized by the disturbing story that was unfolding in front of them.

Each pair of the defendants' parents sat quietly apart from each other as they too focused on the testimony.

As Odom continued to speak his soft Southwestern drawl—still evident thirty years after leaving Dallas—seemed to be almost mesmerizing the court.

After completing his account of how Elyse died that warm July night, Odom also disclosed that a friend of Delashmutt and Fiorella told him that Fiorella had said he committed ''the ultimate sin to God'' and that ''they had bought their ticket to hell.''

However, Delashmutt gave a completely different account to police. He claimed that Elyse Pahler was sitting on a fence when the LSD took effect. She became disorientated and fell forward onto her head.

He then claimed the group was too far from anywhere to get medical attention, and that the three of them feared they'd get into trouble because they had given her the drugs. They stabbed her to death to stop her suffering.

But Odom testified that forensic pathologists had found no evidence of any fractures to the neck or skull that would indicate a life-threatening injury. In addition, it was found that none of the knife wounds separately were enough to cause death.

Forensic experts actually concluded that Elyse slowly bled to death from multiple knife wounds. Prosecutor Dodie Harman used the medical conclusion and the report of the strangulation to support her charge of torture against the two remaining defendants.

Delashmutt's lawyer, Jeffrey S. Yanuk, indicated that his client was considering the prosecution's plea agreement. "Right now our client is not in a position to accept this offer. He has time to think about it."

Then another investigator for the local DA's office, Rick Conradi, described to the court how he discovered that Delashmutt actually told one of his fellow students at Arroyo Grande High School he had had sex with Elyse's corpse.

The youth told investigator Conradi he and Delashmutt were talking about death metal music when Delashmutt began referring to Elyse Pahler. Delashmutt then told his friend how he and the two others used a belt to choke her and then stabbed her repeatedly.

"Delashmutt said they had sexual intercourse with her before she died and after she died," Conradi testified.

The investigator also revealed that Delashmutt even admitted that "frequently" after that, "they would return to her body and have sex with her."

Another investigator told the court that Joseph Fior-ella's mother told him that her son admitted after his arrest that he and Casey both had sex with the girl after she was stabbed.

In early March, 1997, Joseph Fiorella appeared once more before Superior Court Judge Christopher G. Money for sentencing following his guilty plea.

Before deciding on a suitable punishment, the judge allowed the parents and grandparents of Elyse Pahler to speak in aching and, at times, angry voices about the schoolgirl's death.

Elyse's father, David Pahler, addressed Fiorella directly as the courtroom fell into a hushed silence.

"Joseph, it's a parent's worst fear and lifetime pain to outlive their child.

"It's even worse knowing that she was murdered, tortured, and raped as a virgin sacrificed on the altar of Satan so that (you) can earn a ticket to hell."

Fiorella stood completely still, his pale cheeks aflame. His eyes were snapping around the courtroom, studiously avoiding eye-to-eye contact with the family of his victim.

Then Elyse's grandfather, Richard Walter, stood up and once again made a reference to the case's alleged satanic links. Fiorella leaned toward his lawyer and muttered, "That's bullshit."

His outburst was somehow inaudible to the Pahler family. There was no reaction.

Mr. Walter even referred to evidence that some people knew of Elyse's fate before her body was found. He mentioned a more recent case of another missing teenage girl, and implored anyone with knowledge of her whereabouts to come forward.

Not surprisingly, Elyse's family all eulogized the fifteen-year-old schoolgirl as a loving person, and agonized about enduring what her mother called "the hate and the blame and the evil."

"I refuse to focus on the evil that has occurred from this," Lisanne Pahler said in a quiet voice as the rest of her family listened avidly.

"I choose not to dwell on the hate and the blame and the evil. I only choose for him, forgiveness," she said of Fiorella.

Then came a reference that eerily reminded the court that Casey had told investigators soon after his arrest that the boys had chosen Elyse as a "perfect sacrifice to the devil (because) she had blond hair and blue eyes and because she was a virgin . . ."

Her mother Lisanne recalled looking into her newborn daughter's eyes for the first time, and said Fiorella stripped her of that "unconditional love that you can only feel for a child."

And Elyse's father David earlier spoke of his daughter's eyes looking at him only hours before she was murdered, when he said good night and "she said she loved me."

Then, close to tears, he said, "I apologize to my family for not protecting Elyse, for not protecting her from the evil."

Elyse Walter, the loving grandmother, echoed her daughter's carefully chosen words, even as she referred to Fiorella as a "predatory monster."

"We have no vengeance, no hate," she told the court, holding framed photos of Elyse in a soccer uniform and another of her standing next to a snowman. "If we were to have this in our heart, it would be a disservice to this beautiful, beautiful girl."

Minutes later, Fiorella was sentenced to twenty-six years to life for the murder of Elyse Pahler. His lawyer David Hurst had earlier reminded the judge that his client was pleading guilty only to murder and didn't admit to charges of rape and torture.

The term was part of the agreement in which prosecutors dismissed the other charges against the youth in exchange for his guilty plea to first-degree murder.

Only as Joseph Fiorella left the courtroom did he actually allow his eyes to settle for an extended time on the Pahler family. But there were no obvious signs of remorse.

Later, outside the court, defending counsel Hurst admitted that Fiorella had been disturbed by the comments from the Pahler family, even though the youth had been warned they would be allowed to have their say.

"He still wasn't prepared for it when he heard it," said Hurst.

Fiorella was then transferred from county jail to state prison, although he would remain segregated from adult inmates until turning eighteen in June, 1998.

During a subsequent interview with a local newspaper reporter who was trying to prepare a profile on the case, Fiorella—now baby-faced with closely cropped hair and smooth skin, stared coldly from behind the glass window in the jail interview room.

He smirked arrogantly as he explained, "I want to get away from the case. It's no one's business except for my own. I'm not like what they say. I'm just a regular kid."

Asked about his codefendants, he said, "I don't care about them."

He also seemed completely unperturbed by what people might think about the murder.

"It's not like I'm going to be living on the streets," he said with a shrug.

Nor did Fiorella seem bothered by the thought of spending the next two decades of his life in prison. "Whatever happens, happens," he said.

Then, as he prepared to leave the interview room, a more vulnerable look came across his face for a brief moment. "Of course, I feel bad that she's dead."

On Monday, June 23, 1997, a court date was set for July 14 for the preliminary trial of Delashmutt and Casey.

It was also ruled that the two youths would continue to have rape, gang, torture, and conspiracy attached to the murder charges, despite opposition from their defense lawyers.

The most likely date for the full trial to commence was Tuesday, September 23, according to Delashmutt's lawyer Barry Post. The defense counsel also predicted that if the trial did go ahead, it was most likely that only one defendant at a time would be dealt with.

There would be definite advantages to both sides if each defendant had his own trial.

To begin with, the prosecution could use statements by the other defendants that would implicate whoever was on trial. It was also becoming clear that the defense teams behind Delashmutt and Casey had very different strategies.

In September 1997 Royce Casey pleaded guilty to first

degree murder. Other charges against him were dropped. He was expected to be sentenced in mid-November 1997. The trial of Jacob Delashmutt was due to commence by the end of November 1997.

Meanwhile the ordeal would continue for the Pahler family. Their memories of Elyse were being tainted by disturbing court testimony that would relive that appalling night of senseless violence over and over again.

It was as if the nightmare would never end.

Twenty-five

Satan has a much more tenacious grip on the world than many people realize; his power over the human imagination has grown for twenty-two centuries, and in the West even people who deny his existence, or who have no religion at all, live in a culture in which he has a large presence. This demon will not go away.

In ancient Israel, as one sees in early books of the Bible, Satan is hardly the monstrous figure, the dark near parody of God he later became. In the Book of Job, he is the official "opponent" at the heavenly court, his task being to challenge God's assumptions and, with divine permission, to test the fidelity of God's people. But it is no surprise that such a critic should eventually develop into a subverter and a wicked tempter; that transformation was complete by the time the First Book of Chronicles took shape, two centuries before Christ.

During the final centuries B.C., divisions appeared

among the Jews that were to prove fateful to them. One group demonized others: some Jews might not belong. In the second century B.C., the sect called the Essenes arose, and flourished for several centuries. It was among the Essenes that Satan emerged as a necessary evil: "Had Satan not already existed in Jewish tradition, the Essences would have invented him," says author Elaine Pagels in her book *The Origin of Satan*.

Pagels even quotes one of the Essenes scriptures, found among the Dead Sea Scrolls, as saying, "Satan rules in darkness and his purpose is to bring about evil and sin."

The early Christians adopted that view and used much of the same language, seeing themselves as protected by God and angels, freed from satanic manipulation while their antagonists were under diabolical control.

It was these such acute dilemmas that led early Christians to reach so readily for the weapon of demonization. It gave them impetus and assurance, especially when they were up against great opposition. But the demonization of other people accumulated through the centuries at a terrible cost.

Sadly—and some would say inevitably—the most widely accepted claims about satanism in U.S. society today are about teenage involvement in satanic activity. Across the nation these claims are being disseminated chiefly because there seems to be a disturbing link between youth satanism and crime.

Local police talk in regular, disturbing terms about teenage ritualistic crime occurring in numerous communities. Child protection social workers spread the word at conferences about teenage crime.

The truth is that teenagers are drawn gradually into occult ritual activity through interests such as heavy metal music, Dungeons and Dragons fantasy games, and books on occult magic. It is also claimed that many secretive adult satanists encourage these teenagers into black magic ritualism and satanic worship.

Experts believe that once teenagers become obsessed with satanic magic and devil worship, they are driven to commit increasingly serious antisocial acts, such as abusing drugs, vandalizing churches and cemeteries, and killing animals in ritual sacrifices. The next appalling step is suicide, or murder.

As author Pat Pulling asserts in her book, *The Devil's Web*, "Law enforcement officials and mental health professionals now recognize the fact that adolescent occult involvement is progressive. The child who is obsessed with occult entertainment may not stop there, but he often moves on to satanic graffiti and cemetery vandalism. From that point, he easily moves into grave robbing for items needed for occult rituals, and he is just a step away from bloodletting. Bloodletting begins with animal killings and mutilation, and progresses to murder if intervention does not take place."

Dr. Ronald Holmes, professor of criminal justice at the University of Louisville, has even devised a four-step outline that he believes helps identify the essential stages of teenage satanism.

Stage 1. The youth in the occult is immediately drawn into the world of black magic and the worship of the devil because he is told that great worldly power and temporary glory will be his for the asking . . .

Stage 2. The initiate is now exposed to satanic philosophies and becomes one with the demonic belief system . . . This new member learns the prayers, spells, doctrines, dogmas of the faith, holidays, rituals, and the importance of being baptized in the blood of Satan . . .

Stage 3. Now that the youth has progressed into the world of the satanic, he is now accepted into the secret and religious ceremonies of the coven. He learns the various sabbats and the reasons for their celebrations. He participates in the sacrifice for Lucifer . . . The satanist at this level of participation and sophistication with the occult understands the proper animals for sacrifice.

One sacrifice that the new member may become involved with is the human sacrifice. At this stage the member becomes acutely aware that humans are indeed sacrificed for the devil, and the form of sacrifice will take two forms: blood or fire . . .

Stage 4. In the final stage of total involvement in satanism, the young person becomes firmly committed to the occult lifestyle . . .

In the sabbats, the initiate is intimately involved in sexual orgies, which are often an integral part of the worship ceremonies. Obviously, for the seriously disenfranchised members of the youth subculture, this can be a powerful drawing force into full membership.

Often, teenage satanism is linked to satanic groups operated by adults. The Cult Awareness Council of

Houston, Texas, claims ritual child abuse and satanism are connected. A spokesman for the council said:

> "Adult satanists . . . provide an abandoned house for recruits where they engage in drugs, and sex, and listen to allegedly satanic, "heavy metal" music . . . Initially, this is fun for the adolescents. Then, over time, and often while under the influence of some drugs, the recruits are encouraged to engage in various sexual behaviors, and often unbeknownst to them, tapes of their activities are made. These tapes can be marketed as pornography, or they can be used to threaten or blackmail the adolescents into staying with this cult."

In 1990 the Michigan State Police conducted a careful survey of "occult-related" crimes reported by law enforcement agencies in that state. Only 22 percent of the responding agencies reported having investigated any "occult-related" crimes. Almost all of the people who committed such offenses—graffiti, vandalism, the mutilation and killing of domestic or farm animals, and cemetery desecrations, plus 1 percent involving homicides—were young, white males. Only 8 percent of the offenders were over the age of twenty-five and most were teenagers.

Inquiries about the offenders revealed that in almost all cases they were self-taught from sources including friends, heavy metal rock, movies, magazines, and books.

In behavioral science attempts to understand aggressive criminal behavior have led to the identification of two basic kinds of factors that contribute to such behavior:

1. Personality dispositions toward deviant (meaning rule-breaking) aggressive behavior.
2. Group influences upon the person from participation in deviant subcultures that promote criminal behavior.

The beliefs and values that a person uses to justify (to excuse) their aggressive and criminal behavior is usually learned and strengthened in a deviant group subculture. Criminologists refer to these beliefs and values as a "deviant ideology." A deviant ideology functions to neutralize possible feelings of guilt. No particular beliefs are intrinsically deviant. Satanic beliefs can be used as a deviant ideology to justify aggression. So can beliefs about masculine ("macho") pride. Even beliefs about God, Christ, or the Bible can be used as a deviant ideology by some people to justify their aggressive acts.

As author Jeffrey S. Victor points out in his book *Satanic Panic*, "When people justify murder in terms of their personal Christian beliefs, we don't attribute the cause to the Christian religion. Instead we seek the causes of their aggression in their particular personality dispositions and group influences. The same should be done about any vicious act of aggression committed by a teenager, who justifies what he or she has done by referring to some self-taught satanist beliefs. It is misleading to focus too much attention on the excuse of satanist beliefs, no matter how repulsive we might find them.

"The ritual acts and group beliefs of these type of

delinquents does not constitute a religion any more than do the ritual and group beliefs of teenage gang members, or even those of the Ku Klux Klan. It has been well documented that almost all teenagers who profess to be satanists lack any elaborate belief system focused upon devil worship. Instead they have fabricated a deviant ideology in order to justify their underlying personality dispositions to express aggressive hostility, or justify rebellion from adult social restrictions, or obtain public notoriety. This is what I mean when I refer to teenagers as 'pseudo-satanist' delinquents rather than as 'teenage satanists.' ''

In 1991 a careful study of fifty-five so-called teenage pseudo-satanists incarcerated at the Texas Youth Commission Reception Center, in Brownwood, Texas, made some startling conclusions. The delinquents differed from other inmates in several ways:

1. They were virtually all white.
2. They were all from middle-class backgrounds.
3. They had high intelligence scores on IQ tests.
4. They nearly all had used hallucinogenic drugs rather than substances such as cocaine and heroin.
5. They all felt they had little power or control over their lives.
6. Virtually all of them had participated in satanic ceremonies as part of a group activity. None of them could be classified as social loners.

In other words, white, middle-class, highly intelligent teenagers who have a high need for control over their lives are those most likely to justify their criminal activity in terms of a satanist deviant ideology.

In the light of the case highlighted in this book it is a chilling set of findings.

Author Jeffrey S. Victor explains, "The only way to begin to try and curtail this disturbing trend is to understand the underlying psychological causes of such criminal behavior."

Many case studies have provided sensitive portraits of emotionally disturbed teenagers who used satanism to deal with their psychological problems. One case involved a sixteen-year-old, who was undergoing psychotherapy for recurrent depression, severe identity problems, and the abuse of hallucinogenic drugs. The youth first became involved with satanistic ritualism at the age of eleven after attending a "satanic mass" with some friends.

The most common ritual he engaged in was one of his own creation, which he called making proposals. In this ritual he concentrated his thoughts on making a request to the devil to harm someone through his use of mental telepathy. The teenager developed elaborate beliefs around this supposedly magical ritual, involving calling up spirits and demons. The therapist suggested that the boy relied upon this magical thinking and ritualism in order to obtain feelings of power and control in his life.

Satanic Panic author Jeffrey S. Victor adds, "Make-shift black magic rituals offer the excitement of getting away with socially tabooed, deviant behavior, assaulting the moral order of conventional society, and bonding adolescents together in a secret, forbidden activity. The satanistic behavior provides teenagers, who suffer from severe feelings of powerlessness, with an ersatz sense of empowerment.''

Intriguingly, another recent research study of teenagers involved in satanism pointed out the following:

"Once the boys acquired an image of themselves as deviants, they selected new friends who affirmed that self-image. As that self-conception became more firmly entrenched, they also became willing to try new and more extreme deviances. With their growing alienation came freer expression of disrespect and hostility for the representatives of the legitimate society. The disrespect increased the community's negativism, perpetuating the entire process of commitment to deviance.''

Sociologists call this gradual process the development of a deviant identity. They say the process can begin at a very early age, long before adolescents become involved in any serious criminal activity. A child's concept of being a "bad kid" emerges gradually, as a result of experiencing constant humiliations, insults, and rejection at the hands of others. There is abundant research showing that aggressive teenagers experienced more frequent humiliations—from parents, peers, and teachers—to their self-esteem during childhood than nondelinquents.

So-called bad kids attract a circle of friends with similar self-concepts, which is preferable to being socially isolated. Bad kids also often have the power to scare "good kids" simply by their reputations. Ultimately, choosing the self-image of being a bad kid is preferable to having an ambiguous, ill-defined identity.

In a few children, the self-concept of being a bad kid can lead to the child regarding themselves as being "evil." This often happens when children have authoritarian, punitive parents, who use religious threats to humiliate and control them.

Psychotherapist Michael Beck explains how some people who develop an "evil" self-image can lead themselves to believe that their behavior is controlled by the devil.

> "With even more damaged patients who think they are evil, the issue of their ability to deal with anger becomes a priority. They often turn their anger against themselves. The extreme is the patient who becomes totally or partially identified with evil and feels that she or he is either Jesus Christ or the devil, or possibly believes the devil is controlling him or her."

These observations by Michael provide a fascinating insight into why some teenage delinquents may be drawn to satanic beliefs, in order to justify their aggressive behavior. Adolescents who see themselves as being "evil" create a psychological environment consistent with their self-concept. They see the world as they see themselves, a place where malicious evil is more genuine than compassion.

There seems little doubt that the more attention given to the dangers of satanism among the young, the more curious aggression-prone teenagers become about it, and the more some of them start to dabble in it.

It has also clearly emerged that many of today's teenagers live a rootless existence, and those circumstances often draw them together into satanistic behavior. Significantly, more and more middle-class adolescents are experiencing this reaction to their lives.

Many experts say it is going to get worse. Criminologist Gwynn Nettler says, "Advanced, industrial societies like the United States are producing more and more unwanted youth from fragmented families, children who are disconnected from stabilizing adult influences."

One carefully researched report about satanism among young people for teachers and school administrators in the United States concluded:

"Satanic beliefs, when coupled with deviancy, is an outcome of something more basic. In most cases, both the satanic beliefs and the deviancy are symptoms of more fundamental personal problems. A symptom is not a cause. Thus, personal problems, rather than satanic beliefs, should be the target for school or community intervention.

"In fact, any school intervention that narrowly defines its purposes as an effort to purge satanic beliefs from the student body is inappropriate. Such activity is more likely to make satanism attractive. A far more prudent choice is for schools to build programs designed to help overcome personal problems such as substance abuse, academic failure, low self-esteem, child abuse, suicidal tendencies, or a pervasive sense of alienation. Inappropriate concerns over satanic activity may serve to distract educators from developing programs that address serious problems known to affect many students."

Undoubtedly, many teenagers who aspire to be satanists are responding with rage to their own self-hatred. It is a self-hatred born out of lives empty of the love that heals. Perhaps the most malignant evil of our time is the harm caused by neglect and indifference, in societies offering abundant material satisfactions at the cost of poverty in human relationships.

Many have concluded that teenager satanists are those disconnected from loving and caring parents and/or are ostracized from conventional middle-class peers at school. They are likely to experience themselves inhabiting a hostile, uncaring world, in which people's maliciousness is more real than their love. For them, evil is more real than goodness.

Epilogue

In a perfect world, the answers to the wrenching questions of what went wrong in the lives of Royce Casey, Jacob Delashmutt, and Joe Fiorella would be easy to discern. Of course, in a perfect world there would be no real need for answers, because their lives would have been lived out unblemished by the ravenous cancers of hopelessness and hatred.

Sadly, the world is far from perfect, and answers seldom come so effortlessly. In fact, even those first, simple questions—Why did they do what they did? How could they do what they did?—take on new and previously unimagined proportions when one stops to take a closer look, like the eye of a fly magnified ten thousand times. In the end we discover that not only are there no simple answers, there are not even any simple questions.

The long, dark journey of Casey, Delashmutt, and Fiorella began where all such journeys begin—in a place and time of purest innocence, surrounded by the redeeming light of goodness and hope. They were children not unlike the multitude that came before or followed after in the unbroken circle of infinity. Yet before the shadows of these three children's days could lengthen into springtime, each was snatched away by a malevolent undertow of problems. Others have been trapped in those same or even darker waters and somehow survived; still, they gasped for breath and then breathed no more, pulled to their graves by the rolling, sinister waves.

We can easily stand and point an accusing finger at any number of accomplices in the case of Casey, Delashmutt, and Fiorella: a system that failed and allowed them all to slip through its ragged cracks; teachers, doctors, and families who possibly could have but didn't intervene when there was still time and hope.

But all of this seems to leave us no closer to finding answers to the "whys" hidden within the savage murder of Elyse Pahler.

Or perhaps . . . just perhaps . . . there is a pattern here, a common note flowing through the sorrowful, angry requiem for her death. The writer Amos Oz says that "whoever ignores the existence of varying degrees of evil is bound to become a servant of evil." Certainly, one cannot discount the presence of evil here: the evil of the killing itself, the evil that had lain dormant and then exploded within the three teenagers that murderous day in July, 1995. But such evil neither grows nor can it survive in a vacuum. It must first be planted, then nourished and nurtured and helped to come into its full flower by other hands, other wills.

One of those seeds is named silence.

Silence is woven like a sinister web through the sagas of Casey Delashmutt, and Fiorella, three former innocents who finally exploded in fury at someone just as innocent as they had once been. Seeping into every crevice of their lives like cyanide gas, silence became the prison from which there was no escape, the wall through which no one could enter. None of these youths had the voice to break the silence, to tell of the demons raging within . . . while those around them were too deaf to hear their muted cries. Until Casey's conscience broke.

Sadly, these three were far from alone. Fear, loathing, and a lack of moral appreciation are like a mass epidemic that lies barely contained under the onionlike skin of society. Pick any day in any month in any season, and a million children in this nation will be suffering from the same social diseases.

Yet like Royce Casey, Jacob Delashmutt, and Joe Fiorella, most of these children never feel safe enough to speak aloud about their real feelings and lack of guidance, believing that even if there were someone there to listen, no one would hear. No one would care.

The evil that allowed three children to mercilessly rob Elyse Pahler of her life is called silence. Not the renewing, peaceful silence found deep inside a greening forest, or the tender silence of a mother suckling her newborn child—rather, it is that darker and far more ominous silence we maintain about humanity's painful inhumanity toward itself. It is a silence we keep because that inhumanity touches us too profoundly, pains us too deeply, or frightens us too terribly to reveal . . . and because in confronting the truths about that inhumanity, we are forced to confront our own fears—and through those fears, ourselves.

As a society and a human family, we have paid far too high a price for our deafness and speechlessness. We can no longer afford to ignore those unvoiced secrets and unseen wounds that persevere as great unmentionables and ensnare us all in that net of silence from which there is little chance for escape.

There is much we must do. We must find the courage to speak aloud those things that before were only the barest, most terrified whispers of the soul. We must find a way to acknowledge the victims who live among us, and then admit to our own vulnerability. And we must be ready to extend our compassion to the ones who suffer, to help them break the deadly circle of silence before it destroys their lives and society as well.

Finally, we must be willing to confront one last monster from the darkness: our own unspoken fear that in searching for the wellsprings of inhumanity, we might just encounter something of ourselves.

Postscript

It would be reassuring to believe that murder was a gross abnormality, a dramatic departure from respected ethical standards that restrain civilized man from surrendering to his basic instincts. Once, murder was considered to be beyond the pale, irreconcilable with the rest of mankind. But now advances made in our knowledge of ethology, evolution, and human psychology present challenges to such banal assumptions that cannot be ignored. Unfortunately, as man has become more civilized, intelligent, creative, and dominant, so has he become more murderous.

Statistically, murder is still rare in proportion to the population. So the type of crimes allegedly committed by Jacob Delashmutt, Royce Casey, and Joe Fiorella are baffling as none of them fitted—on the surface—the profile of a classic alleged killer.

Murder is a purposive deed that, by horrid paradox,

enables a murderer to reach previously nonexistent levels of violence. Yet that very act often makes him or her despicable to the rest of us, but renders him healthy and admirable in his or her own eyes.

Author Brian Masters studied in great depth the motivation of many notorious killers, and he concluded: "It is hardly surprising that the murderer is reluctant to show remorse for his (or her) acts. It would be a retrograde step, a kind of psychological suicide . . ."

As W. H. Auden wrote:

> *Do not imagine we do not know*
> *Or that what you hide with care won't show*
> *at a glance*

Meanwhile the many individuals affected by the death of Elyse Pahler continue to try and put the tragedy behind them:

DAVID AND LISANNE PAHLER are now living with their three other children in San Luis Obispo. They will probably never recover from their daughter's brutal death. They still don't really know what happened on that hot, humid summer's night in July, 1995. Despite intensive counseling, understandably they have not really managed to come to terms with Elyse's murder.

ELYSE NEILSON WALTER is just as heartbroken by her granddaughter's death. She would like to see the death penalty for teenagers in California and says that the family will take the pain and anguish of Elyse's death to their own graves.

SHANNON PLOTNER is working hard to try and get to college. But she admits there is not a day that goes by when she doesn't think about her great friend Elyse.

ANGEL KATYRYNI has remained close to Shannon, and since Elyse's death they have become reluctant to go out alone in Arroyo Grande. Both Angel and Shannon still keep expecting Elyse to walk through the door one day and tell them about her adventures. They saw *Interview With the Vampire* on cable TV recently, but it wasn't the same without Elyse by their side. "It's hard to explain how I feel about Elyse's death because I still can't quite accept it," says Angel.

JOE FIORELLA and JACOB DELASHMUTT remain friends despite being kept apart in their cells at the San Luis Obispo County Jail. After Joe Fiorella's plea of guilty, he received a 26-year-to-life sentence.

ROYCE CASEY is regularly visited by a minister from the New Life Ministry, in Pismo Beach. He is kept away from the other two defendants, following his decision to plead guilty to being involved in the killing of Elyse Pahler. His sentence had not yet been confirmed at the time of this writing.

SHERIFF ED WILLIAMS continues to keep a tight rein on the case, refusing to elaborate on the evidence against the three suspects.

Prosecutors DODIE HARMAN and DAN BOUCHARD are also reluctant to discuss the case in advance of the remaining trial, but they and their investigators have spent a lot of time interviewing school friends of Elyse and her three alleged killers.

Pahler family attorney ALLAN HUTKIN was prevented from forging ahead with the claim against death metal band Slayer because of the slow progress of the criminal cases against the three youths.

Journalist TOM PARSONS kept a close eye on the progress of the case until June of 1997, when he took up a new position in the public-relations department of an Arroyo Grande bank. But he still predicts that when the remaining defendant finally goes to trial "a lot of people in this town are going to get a big shock."

Photographer ROBERT DYER continues following the case and remains haunted by the sight of that eucalyptus grove where Elyse's body was left to rot under the scorching Californian sun.

"I saw her face. I kept seeing her face. It affected me. Doesn't it affect you? We all knew her, right? And there she is, dead, right there in front of us. We're that close we don't feel like we've lost anything.

"I couldn't even cry for her.

"Sometimes I think it would be a lot easier being dead.

"That's shit."

—*River's Edge*, starring Keanu Reeves, 1986.

About the Author

WENSLEY CLARKSON has written twenty books—which have sold in more than a dozen countries worldwide—including the tabloid newspaper exposé *Dog Eat Dog*, biographies of Hollywood stars John Travolta and Quentin Tarantino, plus ten best-selling true crime books including *Doctors of Death*, *Whatever Mother Says*, *Deadly Seduction*, and *Slave Girls*.

A HANDSOME OVERACHIEVER AND A BEAUTIFUL
HONORS STUDENT MADE THE ULTIMATE LOVE PACT...
MURDER.

BLIND LOVE

THE TRUE STORY OF THE TEXAS CADET MURDERS

PETER MEYER
Author of The Yale Murder

Nothing could come between high school sweethearts
Diane Zamora and David Graham—but something did:
beautiful blonde sophomore Adrianne Jones. After she and
Graham had a sexual encounter, a tearful Graham confessed everything to Zamora. Enraged and out-of-control,
Diane Zamora insisted that there was only one way to
restore the "purity" of their love...so together they murdered Adrianne in an isolated spot outside of their home-
town of Mansfield, Texas. There were no suspects in the
murder until months later, when Diane confessed the crime
to her military school roommates, shocking friends, family, and a picturesque Texas town...

SHE LOVED HER SONS...TO DEATH.

Hush Little Babies

THE TRUE STORY OF A MOTHER WHO MURDERED HER CHILDREN

DON DAVIS

Not since the Susan Smith case has a murder so shocked the nation: a beautiful, loving mother is horrified to find her two young sons stabbed to death on her living room floor by an intruder. Hearts go out to poor Darlie Routier, who appeared to live for her children. But overwhelming evidence soon finds Darlie, the neighborhood's "Most Wonderful Mom," guilty of slaying her own innocent children in cold blood...